HOMESCHOOLING

Guide on How to Homeschool Your Child and Teach Your Child With Confidence

(Practical Support and Encouragement for Learning)

Maria Adams

Published by Oliver Leish

Maria Adams

All Rights Reserved

Homeschooling: Guide on How to Homeschool Your Child and Teach Your Child With Confidence (Practical Support and Encouragement for Learning)

ISBN 978-1-77485-123-4

All rights reserved. No part of this guide may be reproduced in any form without permission in writing from the publisher except in the case of brief quotations embodied in critical articles or reviews.

Legal & Disclaimer

The information contained in this book is not designed to replace or take the place of any form of medicine or professional medical advice. The information in this book has been provided for educational and entertainment purposes only.

The information contained in this book has been compiled from sources deemed reliable, and it is accurate to the best of the Author's knowledge; however, the Author cannot guarantee its accuracy and validity and cannot be held liable for any errors or omissions. Changes are periodically made to this book. You must consult your doctor or get professional medical advice before using any of the suggested remedies, techniques, or information in this book.

Upon using the information contained in this book, you agree to hold harmless the Author from and against any damages, costs, and expenses, including any legal fees potentially resulting from the application of any of the information provided by this guide. This disclaimer applies to any damages or injury caused by the use and application, whether directly or indirectly, of any advice or information presented, whether for breach of contract, tort, negligence, personal injury, criminal intent, or under any other cause of action.

You agree to accept all risks of using the information presented inside this book. You need to consult a professional medical practitioner in order to ensure you are both able and healthy enough to participate in this program.

Table of Contents

INTRODUCTION 1

CHAPTER 1: HOMESCHOOLS, HOW LEGAL IS IT....REALLY?. 2

CHAPTER 2: IS HOMESCHOOLING RIGHT FOR YOUR FAMILY? 13

CHAPTER 3: HOW HOMESCHOOLING CAN HELP YOU LAUNCH YOUR CAREER (BEFORE COLLEGE) 26

CHAPTER 4: FIRST THINGS FIRST: UNDERSTAND YOUR PHILOSOPHY 33

CHAPTER 5: WHY DO YOU WANT TO HOMESCHOOL? 42

CHAPTER 6: WHAT IS HOMESCHOOLING? 51

CHAPTER 7: 10 TIPS FOR TEACHING READING 67

CHAPTER 8: WHAT IS HOMESCHOOLING? 78

CHAPTER 9: THE ADVANTAGES OF HOME SCHOOLING AND ROAD SCHOOLING 86

CHAPTER 10: SPIRITUAL PREPARATION FOR HOMESCHOOLING 94

CHAPTER 11: RECENT GROWTH & ACCEPTANCE OF HOMESCHOOLING 118

CHAPTER 12: HOMESCHOOLING IS EDUCATION THAT IS TAILOR-FITTED TO YOUR CHILDREN'S SPECIFIC TEMPERAMENTS, BODY CLOCKS, AND LEARNING STYLES. 125

CHAPTER 13: HOW TO CREATE LESSON PLANS 129

CHAPTER 14: HOMESCHOOLING YOUR PRESCHOOLER .. 141

CHAPTER 15: INVALUABLE RESOURCES: HOMESCHOOL CONVENTIONS, CO-OPS, CAMPS, LEADERSHIP SCHOOLS 144

CHAPTER 16: GUIDELINES FOR DISCIPLINE IN HOMESCHOOLING AND TEENAGERS. 149

CHAPTER 17: ROUTINES FOR HOMESCHOOLING 160

CHAPTER 18: PARENTS ARE THE BEST ROLE MODELS. ... 167

CHAPTER 19: HOMESCHOOLING - ARE THERE OTHER OPTIONS? 173

CONCLUSION 182

Introduction

This book contains the necessary information you need to know on how to start homeschooling your child. If you have concerns or doubts, you will find in this book the answers you need. You can learn about the benefits of homeschooling, how it differs from sending your child to school, and what you can do to make it as fun and effective as possible.

If you're worried about where to start, this book will guide you through the things you need to know. Teaching methods and tips are also included to help you and your child tackle the challenges of homeschooling efficiently.

Chapter 1: Homeschools, How Legal Is It....Really?

So this little book can be busted in the first sentence. We have touched on this in the introduction. Is this whole thing called homeschooling even legal? Must teachers not have diplomas and degrees to practice?

The short answer is this:

Homeschooling and becoming the primary teacher for your child is 100% legal.

Again, we urge you to commit in finding out from your State, what their specific rules and regulations are. However we are sure that Homeschooling is 100% legal in all States of the US. International readers, there are few modern western countries that this is not legal, but again find out from your educational administrators.

Law makers regulating it vary and it also changes from time to time. But nothing prevents you to homeschool your children. I want to repeat that so that it sinks in...

Nothing can prevent you from taking control of your child's precious future through homeschooling.

The National Home Education network is a wonderful resource when it comes to the legalities of homeschooling, and you can visit their website here: http://www1.nhen.org/

As a main theme throughout this booklet, we will urge you to do your homework. There are so many websites and information available. Don't get overwhelmed, but search and learn. Get the facts.

Now that we know it is perfectly legal a next pressing question emerges. Why would you even consider homeschooling?

This we will try and answer with a look at some advantages of homeschooling and the major disadvantages of the public school system. Hopefully, this will assist you in making up your mind. Again this list is not complete and please if it does not convince you, then please look and research further.

The Pros of homeschooling

It is imperative that you make an informed decision about homeschooling. I don't want to fluff it with allot of words. Time to get straight to the point. So here are my list (and there might be thousands of other reasons as well) of why you should seriously entertain the thought of homeschooling.

Time management. The scenario in each home across the country, no, the world, is the same every single morning. You wake up, shout everyone out of bed, rush, rush, and rush only to sit in traffic and then maybe late, dropping your kids at school. Now, you might look at this first reason with a sense of skepticism. How can time management be the first and foremost reason to start homeschooling? Come on! What happened to actual learning!

Well, I have this philosophy. It is nothing new, just thought I should throw that in the equation. The only thing that cannot be – and yes love can be – bought is time. Imagine the opposite. Imagine waking rested, your children waking rested. Have a nice sit-down breakfast where you can plan your day. That is priceless. It is priceless time spent with the most important people in your life.

Time is everything the most precious commodity in the world. Once it passed it is gone forever.

That is why this one is at the top of the list!

Homeschooling gives parents control over the moral and religious upbringing of their children. Listen, this booklet does not preach any moral or religious conviction. Neither do we attempt to debate whether it is morally correct bestowing your convictions on your children. But we live in a world where this is becoming secular. If this is important to you, Homeschooling is the only way you will be able to bring your children up in your belief and moral values.

For most people this might be top of the list. Individual attention. I won't go in to much detail – it is delightfully obvious – but so misunderstood. Not all children are the same. In facts siblings differ night and day. That means children's ability to learn, to be taught differs night and day. Now why do we want to force children into conformity of learning? And sorry, no matter how well prepared a public or even private school system says they can give individual attention, it is simply not possible for them. They cannot give that type of attention to and for your child. Not like in a homeschooling setup.

Homeschooling is the only way we can develop children for the demands of the new world. Bold statement. But this one can hit the core of it. We live in an ever increasing and demanding world. Yet, we have a formal education system that does not address this and is geared towards an old "professional" developing and linear learning approach. In fact, I am confident we are setting up our children to fail. So why would we do it? Why would we not give our children the absolute best chance of functioning and becoming successful for the demands of a new world?

Can I be frank with you for one second? I wish I can elaborate on this part and get stuck into more detail. If you for one moment think the world will become a less demanding, complicated and competitive environment then think again. It won't. It can't and it will never. It will become even more tough and only through homeschooling, through teaching our children survival techniques will we ever be able to get them ready for the demands of such a world.

Just think about emotional development. How many emphasis is necessary? In fact, the so called soft skills is the one's neglected by public schools, yet it is the most essential to actually survive in a modern world. Does schools teach stress management? Time management? Well if you for one second think that stress will be less in twenty years' time...think again! What about neuro linguistic programming – the one thing that will guard us and our emotional state in the future? What about goal setting? Productivity? Family responsibility? Finding your true purpose? The list goes on and on. Yet schools will still focus on the main, out of date, subjects and curriculums, throwing a halfhearted period of development studies into it. It is not enough. We want our children to cope and survive but above all be well balanced successful members of society.

There are less competition and negative peer pressure. Proponents that criticize homeschooling will always throw the socializing card in front of you. That, through homeschooling you take children out of the real world. Honestly what a bunch of stupid (I have other words...lol). Nothing could be further from the truth. Through homeschooling you can actually take negative peer pressure away. In a less competitive environment your child can learn at his/her own pace. And you can make time for social activities.

Allows time for children with a special talent to be fully developed. You might have a child that has a special talent for a specific sport, art or intellect. Homeschooling will allow structured time where in public school this will only be an extra afterschool activity.

Disadvantages of Homeschooling

Well... surprise, surprise...

There is none – at least to my honest opinion.

The only disadvantage might be if you as a parent is not up to task or does not have the ability to leave your job.

Myths of public schooling

Do not get me wrong. The public school system is not doom and gloom and if, after the end of reading this booklet, homeschooling still does not resonates with you, then it does not mean your child will be lost.

There is still allot you can and should do to supplement the shortcomings of public school and develop the well balanced people of the future.

If it can't, it can't, but it is important to dispel some popular myths about public schooling.

Socializing as we touched on earlier is still hailed as the greatest advantage of sending your child to public school. There is some truth to the statement, however, the biggest myth is that no one takes into account that a child then can only interact with peers. Neuro science has taught us that through the power of mirror neurons our children are t programmed to accept their peer reality as the only reality. Big words. Bold statement. But the truth. The fact is children rarely socialize outside the peer group. Almost never with adults.

Homeschooling, through creative innovation and planning, can change this with scheduled and natural interaction on all fronts. There are many patents which homeschools' their children. And that opens social events. You can let your child join community groups, let them work as volunteers, exposing them to an array of socializing capabilities.

This statement will give me the biggest criticism from formal public school educators. However, it is worth mentioning again. We are not creating children capable to handle themselves for the demands of the future. Structured leering to pass an exam is outdated.

Teaching children that academic education is the only way for success, thus neglecting softer emotional skills is also outdated. There is in fact no reason a person should ever go through public school unless you want to become a "professional" IE and accountant, lawyer or engineer. Schools only prepare people for that.

We hope these few pros and cons and myths have helped you to make an informed decision. Since the decision to homeschool is one of the biggest you will ever make as a parent, we urge you to read the last section again. Also please do further reading.

In the next section we will start to examine the ABC's of homeschooling. What you can expect and some of the tips and tricks of the trade.

Chapter 2: Is Homeschooling Right For Your Family?

Parents choose to homeschool their children for many reasons. Many families cannot afford to purchase uniforms or large quantities of supplies due to the rising cost of public schools.

Bullying is a growing problem in schools. If your child is not in the same category, they can be targeted. Unfortunately, teachers, school counselors, and principals cannot do anything about it - or so they claim.

Another reason to homeschool is the high level of education available in many schools. Because they are filled with students who have no interest learning, many teachers in schools are just glorified babysitters. This list could go on.

No matter what your reasons for homeschooling are, there are some things you should consider before you make that final decision.

Take a look at this checklist to see where you stand regarding homeschooling.

* Find out about the laws that govern homeschooling in your area. It can be very easy or difficult to homeschool your children depending on where you live. Many states have laws that require parents to hold a degree in teaching before their children can be homeschooled.

Others require that you register your child in the local school district and declare your intention to homeschool. While some areas will require you to keep track of attendance and report it, others do not. You can avoid trouble by checking the laws in your area.

The Beginner's Guide to Professional Homeschooling

* Try to be patient. There are many children who, despite being loved by their

parents and showing difficult and challenging behavior. These children's parents are often relieved when their children go to school. This is the only way these parents can take a breather. It's therefore important to assess how patient you are.

Are you able to have patience with your child? You will also need patience to help your child understand something they may not grasp the first time. These situations require you to be calm.

* Make learning enjoyable: There are many teachers who have been trained but don't know this one. This is a crucial requirement for homeschooling. This is something that many parents can do better than teachers. Your imagination and creativity can help you inspire your children to learn.

* Are you qualified to teach your children? This is a tough question, but it doesn't have the power to stop you. Even if you

struggled with a particular subject in school, it can be an opportunity to help your children understand and learn more about the topic.

This list will help you decide if homeschooling is right for you. This is the beginning of a rewarding, fulfilling and fun adventure.

The Beginners Guide to Professional Homeschooling

Socialization and Homeschooling

Although it is a tired topic the subject of homeschooling and socialization will continue to be discussed. This is especially important for children who don't have siblings or with siblings they don't get along. Everyone needs to be able to socialize with others to have a happy childhood.

Parents of homeschooled kids find ways to make it happen. Some parents struggle with this aspect of homeschooling, though, because they have always relied on the public school system to give their children friendships.

It is important to ensure that your children have the opportunity to meet new friends once you start homeschooling them. The problem might be solved for families who attend church regularly. Many churches have youth activities. This can often provide enough social exposure for your children to make great friends.

Outside activities, such as dance or martial arts classes, are another way to expose your children to other kids. Any activity that allows your child to interact with other children is a great way for them to make new friends. You can also give your children entertainment and let them learn a new skill.

There are likely to be other children in your neighborhood that you can socialize with. You can invite the children of the neighborhood to a party by using special occasions such as birthdays. This can be great fun for all and your child may make new friends by the end.

The Beginners Guide to Professional Homeschooling

Do not let your children believe that they won't make friends if they are homeschooled. Children are more likely to make friends if they're left alone. Take them on a vacation to the beach for one week. They'll be able to make friends quickly the moment they arrive, and they will continue to spend the week with their friends. Children are stronger than we give them credit for.

You don't have to worry about whether your children will be friends if they are homeschooled. They will do fine without you. They just need to be curious about other children and that's it. If your children aren't as social as they should, you might want to help them by setting up some activities so that they can make new friends.

Participating in Sport with Your Homeschooled Child

Many parents worry about whether their children will be able participate in sports when homeschooling their children. This can be overcome if your child enjoys playing sports. It all depends on the sport that your child is most interested in.

If your child is more interested in a single sport like tennis or golf, it's easy to find a way to allow him or her to play that sport. You can find instructors who are qualified to teach both these sports. Private lessons can be given weekly, daily, or every other day during the week. Your kids will have more chances to compete if you are a member of a country or similar club.

You don't have to join a club, but you can contact your local YMCA/YWCA to find out which programs they offer that your children could be involved in. Many offer softball, swimming, and other team sports that your child can participate in. They can participate in their favorite sport for several weeks for a small fee.

The Beginners Guide to Professional Homeschooling

You can also try dancing, martial arts, or gymnastics. Each child is different so you might have to give them a variety of options before finding the one that sparks their interest. There may be many options when it comes sport-related activities.

There's also the possibility that your kids will find a sport they love. You'll need to do some research to find a team that will attract them. It will be more difficult to find a team for them if they are interested in something like basketball or football.

You may even have to stop homeschooling once they reach high school in order for them to be able to participate in the sport they love. If you have done your job well, they should be able handle public schools.

Homeschooling your children can give them more time to learn and practice if they are passionate about a single sport like tennis or golf. Many colleges and universities have teams of golfers. Some schools may offer sports scholarships to students.

For many, gymnastics can be a life-long passion. Gymnasts can even be part of the Olympic team, male and female. Although dancing can be challenging, it can open doors to many opportunities and make a great career.

You can help your child to participate in any sport they are interested in and achieve whatever goal you may set for them.

Homeschooling vs. Unschooling

Once you have made the decision that your children will be taught at home, rather than in a classroom setting,

The Beginners Guide to Professional Homeschooling

You can send them to a regular school but there is another option. It is up to you to decide whether to homeschool or opt for a newer method, called unschooling.

Although there are many differences between these methods, the important thing is that they all work in the same way. Both methods aim to ensure that your children learn things.

Unschooling is a term that school personnel, teachers, and parents who support mainstream teaching methods are uncomfortable with. These people feel that children who are taught this method will not learn as much as they need and will not be able live up to their full potential. Parents who use unschooling to teach their children at the home have many successes.

Unschooling is not fully understood by everyone. Although there are many definitions of this term, the main meaning is that children learn what interests them most. This doesn't necessarily mean that children don't learn anything. It's actually quite the opposite.

Unschooled children learn more than those who are taught in a strict school environment. This method of learning is more effective as the children can choose what they wish to study, without having to follow a lot of rules and regulations.

Forcing them to learn things they don't like.

Most likely, you will never use it in your entire life.

Children will remember what they have learned when they are allowed to explore what interests them. Children who are not educated can still learn the basics of math, writing, and reading. These subjects are taught in fun and interesting ways.

You should first look at the statistics before you criticize the unschooling technique.

The Beginners Guide to Professional Homeschooling

Unschooled children are more likely to be relaxed and eager to learn, simply because they aren't being forced into learning something they don't like. It's quite normal to rebel against something that you don't like, and this is even more true for children.

Children will remember what you teach them if you make them learn it. This is because they are able to score well on tests. But, how much of the memorized material will they remember in a year or a week?

Unschooled children retain more knowledge because they want to learn and are eager to learn. That should be the goal of all teaching methods regardless of their subject matter.

You can incorporate parts of homeschooling and unschooling in your teaching methods to find the perfect solution. You'll find that your children will be enthusiastic and eager to learn, as well as being able to recall what you taught them.

They've been taught for many years.

Chapter 3: How Homeschooling Can Help You Launch Your Career (Before College)

More and more kids these days are starting businesses. With the Internet it's easy to see why.

The web offers a wealth of knowledge right at our fingertips and all kinds of outlets that allow us to get creative and sell our work. Kids all over the world are raking in the dough by selling art, stories, services (like coding), or even products that they make by hand ("Ry's Ruffery" comes to mind – kid is making thousands selling dog treats).

The cool thing about homeschooling is that you can design your education to support an early career, allowing you to stand out in the college application pool, earn money, and gain work experience that will put you far ahead of many college grads by the time you start looking for a job. You might even be lucky enough to earn so much paper that you don't need a job (hey, it's happened before). Either way, if you think you know what you want to do with your life, there's no time like the present to get started.

Don't know what you want to do? Get started anyway.

I had lots of different interests growing up, so I was never really sure about what kind of career I wanted. All I knew was that I liked to write.

I launched dozens of blogs throughout middle school and high school, allowing me to explore lots of different subjects of interest and hone my skills as a writer. I wrote about books, music, philosophy, education, business, marketing, and entrepreneurship. A lot of it was inspired by the things I was studying at the time, and it helped me get a grasp on what my true passions were. This led to my music magazine Mob Sounds (formerly

GuitarTrump) – my first real success as a writer.

Through this site, I managed a staff of six writers who got free press passes to cover great concerts (we're talking legendary bands – Pearl Jam, Joan Jett, and the like). I gained a lot of experience this way as a writer, editor, leader, and communicator – skills which allowed me to start working as an independent contractor at the age of fifteen and start paying off my student loans as soon as I began going to college.

Throughout the process, I was always studying different things to help me get ahead.

I followed successful bloggers and journalists. I read books about social media marketing, business, communication, leadership, and entrepreneurship. I experimented with different marketing and business tactics based on the books that I read and what I learned from studying my competitors.

This led to my mom and I designing courses based off of what I studied outside of school, meaning I got to put all kinds of cool classes on my high school transcript. Things like...

- Writing for Profit I + II
- Entrepreneurship
- Leading a Successful Life
- Leadership
- Social Media Marketing
- Marketing and Promotion

My mom and I modeled my courses so that they were similar to those offered in public institutions as far as time and effort goes while still giving me a lot of say in what I studied. I visited our library every couple of weeks and scouted the web for resources to supplement different areas of study. For example, one of the books I read for my Writing for Profit I course was Darren Rowse's ProBlogger: Secrets for Blogging Your Way to a Six-Figure Income. I then spent 3-6 hours per week experimenting with the tactics I read about until I got through the whole book. I kept track of my hours and the results of my experiments, then I moved onto something new.

Not only was this method of learning a ton of fun, it felt important. I felt like I was in control of my education, that I was learning things I could apply to my career for the rest of my life.

Now, the laws about homeschooling are different according to different states, so you have to be careful with how you go about this. In Florida, there is a lot of freedom in course design. All you have to do is keep samples of your work (called a portfolio) for 2 years, keep a log of all activities as you do them along with a list of all reading materials you use, and complete evaluations annually.

To meet the evaluation requirement you have a choice between having the portfolio evaluated by a teacher who holds a valid regular Florida teaching certificate, taking a nationally normed test administered by a certified teacher, taking a state student assessment test, being evaluated by a psychologist, or any other method allowed by your local school district. We usually met with a teacher for the evaluation. Google homeschooling laws in your area to learn more about the requirements for your individual state.

For me, things didn't have to be too structured. As long as I put in 20-30 hours per week studying and working/experimenting (and kept a log of my progress), I was able to improvise throughout the year.

This made the process less stressful and much more effective than if we had come up with a rigid schedule at the beginning of the year. I was learning things at my own pace and could move on to different areas of study as it made sense based on my progress.

After all, the world of business and marketing is constantly evolving thanks to the Internet. Different ideas and tactics can quickly become outdated, so it's nice to have some flexibility as things change (this was especially true for social media marketing).

Of course, I didn't go about all of my classes this way, and there's a good (albeit dumb) reason for that...

Chapter 4: First Things First: Understand Your Philosophy

Opting not to enroll your child in a traditional school must have been a decision you agonized over and made for good reasons; whatever these reasons may be is not the purpose of this guide. We trust you have considered all options available and decided that homeschooling your child is in your and your child's best interest.

Since you probably don't like the traditional approach to education, you definitely don't not want to replicate a classroom setting at home. To create a homeschooling curriculum for your child, one that suits and addresses his/her needs and requirements, and one that helps him or her grow into a confident, responsible, intelligent, and smart adult, you need to understand your philosophy first, which you can do by:

Being clear on what homeschooling is and is not

A common misconception held by many parents is that homeschooling means exclusively teaching your child from a home setting or personally teaching him/her every subject. This is far from true. Homeschooling does not limit itself to a home setting or the parent as the sole teacher.

It mainly refers to you (the parent) taking direct responsibility and making all important decisions related to your child's education and the content taught to him/her instead of allowing an educational institution to make those decisions for your child.

When you choose to homeschool your child, you accept full responsibility over what your child learns and who will teach him or her certain subjects. This means you can hire tutors to teach your child certain subjects.

Now that you have clarified your understanding of what homeschooling is and is not, seek to understand your philosophy towards it.

Let's talk about that:

Understanding Your Homeschooling Philosophy

Every parent who decides to homeschool his/her kids has a unique philosophy because it revolves around the values and knowledge the parent wants to teach the kids as well as the unique needs of the child. To build an effective curriculum that caters to all your child's educational needs, figure out your homeschooling philosophy.

You need to know and understand what you want and do not want your child to learn and understand at a certain level and grade. For instance, if your child is in grade 2, his/her requirements will be different to that of a child in grade 5 or high school. You need to figure out what you really want your child to learn in a particular grade because this knowledge is what shall help you devise an appropriate curriculum.

Take a notebook and write down important points related to what you think your child should learn at specific points in his or her life, the things you wish to keep away from him/her, and the values you want your child to learn.

You need to be very clear on the different subjects you wish to teach him/her and what topics you wish to cover in each subject at a certain level. For instance, if you plan to teach your child science in grade 1, you need to figure out the extent to which you will be teaching it and the topics you will introduce in the science curriculum.

To understand and figure out your homeschooling philosophy, assess your child's abilities and needs and consider his/her interests and style.

Assess your child's abilities

When homeschooling your kids, the level of grade does not matter much. You can teach your child anything you want at any time you want and for whatever subject you think is right for your kid. For instance, your 7 year old may be better in English as compared to a 10 year old. If that is the case, you'll have to teach him/her English taught at grade 5 or 6. If, for example, you discover that your 8 year old is not ready for the level of mathematics taught in grade 3 and needs to start from the basics, you can do so.

Hence, to devise an appropriate homeschooling curriculum, you need to analyze your child's abilities so you know the level he/she is on and can then create a curriculum that caters to his/her abilities and needs.

However, your child's abilities are not always straight across the board. You may find that one of your children is a science whiz while another leans more towards English literature. In this scenario, it is better if you pick and build a homeschooling curriculum that revolves around the unique abilities of your child rather than be rigid when picking a curriculum and opt for a boxed or pre-packaged curriculum.

Consider your child's interests, passions, and learning style

In addition to understanding your child's abilities, focus on his/her interests, passions, and learning style. Some children learn how to read by playing games like Minecraft whereas some learn concepts through rhymes and songs. Some children understand concepts fast when turned into songs while others understand things better if turned into games and exciting exercises.

When pursuing a balanced and beneficial home education for your children, do not forget to pay attention to your child's interests and learning style. If your child is passionate about playing the piano, it is perfectly fine to encourage him/her to pursue their passion and teach him or her how to become a pianist. You can slowly incorporate other subjects into his/her curriculum as well.

You should never treat homeschooling as a one size fits all approach because if it were, you would not have decided to homeschool your child; instead, you would have sent him or her to a traditional school.

Homeschooling is about being creative and thinking outside the box so you can design a curriculum that suits your child's uniqueness.

To figure out what your child leans the most towards and what he/she is good at, observe your child for a few weeks as he/she engages in different activities. In addition, introduce different ideas, subjects, and activities to him/her as a way to see what attracts him/her and grabs his/her attention.

Analyze the time you can devote to teaching your kids

The other important thing you need to consider is the amount of time you can devote to homeschooling your kids and your own teaching style. Some parents have jobs and businesses to attend to and therefore cannot devote 4 to 5 hours daily to homeschooling kids. Other parents may have more time on their hands and can fully devote it towards homeschooling their kids.

Figure out how much time you can devote daily or weekly to teaching your children. Do you prefer giving them an hour or two every day or is it more convenient for you to teach them for 4 to 5 hours every other day? Also, be clear on your teaching style and the homeschooling type that will suit you and your child.

The following sections highlight the most popular homeschooling approaches; you can pick one and customize it to your child and teaching style keeping in mind the things we have discussed in this section thus far.

Chapter 5: Why Do You Want To Homeschool?

We talked about the current world events and the CDC guidelines in the intro, so now that we've gotten that out of the way let's talk about some of the other reasons you may have chosen to homeschool.

There are so many reasons parents make this decision, here are just a few: *Excessive bullying. *You're unhappy with the current quality of education your child is receiving. *You may be the parent of a special needs child. *You may be relocating mid-year and would like to finish out the year at home. *Maybe a Christ centered education is important to you and you cannot afford private school. *Your child may have had an unfortunate bad experience in a public or private school setting. *Maybe you just feel in your heart it is the right thing to do for your child.

Whatever the reasoning is behind your decision to homeschool the main point to focus on here is that they are YOUR REASONS. You don't owe anyone an explanation on why you've chosen to oversee your child's education at home. You will undoubtedly get a few sideways looks, and raised eyebrows when you announce that you've made this choice for your family. Most people will be very polite even if they disagree with your decision. Most people are adult enough to understand that what works for one person may not work for someone else. Most people will respect that these are your children and their opinion is just that, their opinion.

However...that's only most people. There are the select few that will ask you what makes you think you are qualified to teach your children? Do you have a degree in education? There are the select few that will be adamant that public school works so well for their child it must be great for all children. There are the select few that will completely disrespect your decision and have absolutely nothing positive or encouraging to say. These people are not your people. By that I mean do not expect to win them over, or eventually prove your homeschool success to them. They will always be able to find something to question or criticize.

So what do you do with these select few people that will never understand? Rise above. What would you tell your children to do? Most of us would tell our children that some people will judge you and have harsh opinions of you for no other reason than they just don't understand. We would tell our children to rise above that, and stick to their convictions. When you feel like you are being judged or criticized for your decision to homeschool your child go back to your original reasoning for why you made this decision in the first place.

For myself personally I have not been subject to too many disrespectful opinions. At the time we decided to homeschool our fourth grader, school was let out for Christmas break and he never went back. I was bombarded with a ton of questions. What happened? Did something happen at school? Is he ok? Will he go back? Is this a sure thing? Is this temporary? Do you know what you're doing? How are you going to teach him? Are you qualified to do this? Are you sure this is legal?

These questions bothered and annoyed me a lot at first. I was so busy reassuring myself that I could do this, and this is what I feel in my heart is best for my son. At the same time I was questioning myself. Is this the right choice? Am I making a huge mistake? What if I fail him? What if I can't actually do this? How much math do I remember? I was actually not very good at math at all, oh Lord can I teach him fractions when I don't even remember learning that? It wasn't until I decided to have an automated response that I was able to stop questioning myself every time someone questioned me. I just simply replied with something along the lines of, "After a lot of prayer and thought my husband and I decided this may be a good option for our son. We talked to our son about it, asked him to pray about it too, and here we are. We believe this is where the Lord wants us to be right now, and if a change needs to be made He will show us when and how that needs to happen."

You may not be a praying person, that's ok. The point is to just have a 'go to' response. I call this my blanket response because it covers almost any question on my reasoning to homeschool. It can be as simple as, "We talked this over as a family and decided we were going to give it a try and see how it works out. If it works well we may continue, if it's not the right fit for us we can always go back to public school or try something different."

Now, I have to admit I can be a bit of a sarcastic person, and I have a bit of a dry sense of humor. I have run across people during the day when children are usually in school and gotten the, "Oh, is there no school today?" I respond kindly to this and say, "Oh, we homeschool." Every once in a blue moon I will get a snarky rude comment. It's usually something along the lines of, "Oh, so you must have something against teachers." Or, "Don't you worry your children will be weird when they grow up?" Seriously no joke, I have gotten these questions, IN FRONT OF MY CHILDREN! I again respond kindly, but admittedly sarcastically, "No, I don't have a thing against teachers at all. Teachers are amazing! I'm just doing my part to lessen the class sizes for other people's children." As far as the idea of worrying my children will grow up to be weird, I just respond with, "Sometimes I worry my children will be normal when they grow up, but then I remind myself, I am their mom so there is absolutely no way normal is going to happen. They will definitely be weird. But not because we homeschool."

My children and I have a very healthy ongoing dialogue about how when you go against the "normal standards" you are questioned quite a bit. You can either be bothered and upset by it, or have fun with it. My witty answers are hopefully an example to them of how to let those opinions roll off their shoulders and just have fun with it.

Your reasoning behind your decision to homeschool your child does not need to be discussed in detail unless you choose to do so. You don't owe anyone any explanation on why you have made this choice.

Our extended family has been very supportive of our decision to homeschool. We had a few questions in the beginning, and a bit of concern but nothing offensive or intrusive. I have heard horror stories from other homeschool moms whose family was just down right rejecting the entire idea and belittling their ability as mothers to take on this responsibility. In these cases the most successful ways of maintaining sanity and preserving family relationships is firm boundaries. You may need to have a discussion about where the boundaries are. Decide what you are willing to discuss and what you're not. Stick to your boundaries. Anything that starts to produce thoughts of self doubt does not belong inside the boundaries of discussion.

Take some time to really think about all the reasons you are going to homeschool. Write them down. Every single last reason. Seriously even the small ones. One of my son's reasons behind homeschooling was the simple fact that he found sun butter disgusting and he was looking forward to never seeing it on a lunch tray again.

There's just something about writing down a list of reasons and visually seeing the list grow and grow that reaffirms to ourselves that this is a well thought out logical decision and here are all of the reasons why. Being able to hold it and see it turns it into a tangible validation of your thought process.

Chapter 6: What Is Homeschooling?

Homeschooling occurs when a child gets an education at home rather than in a school setting. Also called home education or home based education, it is facilitated by either the parents themselves or by a private tutor. It is perceived, at times, as the ultimate privatization of education. This is because when homeschooling, parents must secure funding, choose the content of the curriculum, and determine how to grade and progress their child.

Homeschooling has been going on for as long as there have been homes around the world. It is an integral part of the family and the community and has been since the dawn of humanity. In past centuries, children received their education at home from their parents or in the community. There were no schools, or if there were then only the children of the wealthy and powerful could attend. Schools were viewed back then as a privilege and not a necessity. Homeschooling was the only way for most children to receive their education. During those days, education consisted mostly of learning life skills and lessons by doing chores and meeting the daily needs at home. Children were only able to learn how to read and perform basic arithmetic, if they were lucky enough to have parents who knew how to teach them. Some parents would hire a teacher to educate their children. Mostly, these teachers would be given room and board in exchange for teaching the children in the community. In some cases, once a child became old enough, they were sent to an apprenticeship under a local professional, such as blacksmiths, carpenters, doctors, etc. where he or she would learn a trade. Often, these apprenticeships may cost the family a small fortune, which they gladly paid in hopes that the child would become a professional and help the family in the future.

It is only around the 1900s that public schools have become widespread in many countries and available for children from any walk of life. And even then, many parents still chose to educate their children at home for various reasons. Countries eventually adopted laws that made public school attendance mandatory, drastically decreasing the prevalence of homeschooling. In recent decades, there was a growing dissatisfaction among parents regarding public education. In some countries, dissatisfied parents formed movements that favored homeschooling over public education, filing petitions to legalize homeschooling in their Constitutions.

Today, homeschooling is legal in many countries around the world. Countries where homeschooling is prevalent include Australia, New Zealand, Canada, The United Kingdom, and the United States. In Spain, homeschooling is neither legal nor illegal as their Constitution recognizes freedom of education. However, the national education law requires that compulsive education be met through student attendance. On the other hand, Germany, Greece, Macedonia, Bosnia, and Cuba are some of the countries where homeschooling is illegal and public education is mandatory without any exceptions. There are also other countries where homeschooling is not restricted by law, but it is considered socially unacceptable and is virtually non-existent.

Laws regarding homeschooling differ from country to country and state to state. However, one thing is clear; these laws usually take effect when the child is somewhere around the age of seven or eight, or the age where they usually begin school in their country. Prior to that age, the education parents provide at home to their children is of no legal concern to the government. Homeschooling a child prior to his or her school-age usually consists of the basics such as

How to talk, walk, and run

How to sing and play games

How to get dressed and tie shoelaces

How to recognize and recite the alphabet

How to count to 10, 20, and so on

How to write his or her name

While these fundamentals are usually the ones that are taught at home before they begin going to school, it does not mean that these are the only things that can be taught to preschoolers. Some parents also teach their child how to read, do simple math, and learn to play an instrument, all before the child is old enough to attend kindergarten.

Once a child becomes old enough to start school, he or she becomes subject to laws that aim to ensure his or her education. Most children are sent to public or private schools, while some are told to stay at home where their education is set to continue. In a typical homeschool setting, one parent is the breadwinner while the other stays at home to supervise the education process. There are also single-parent families, as well as families whose parents are both working, who also homeschool. In these scenarios, it is often another family member (an aunt, an uncle, or a grandparent) or a tutor who does the teaching.

Why Homeschool?

There are many reasons why some parents opt to homeschool their children. In some cases, parents become encouraged to homeschool their children when they see that he or she responds well to the homeschooling received prior to school age. Because they see encouraging results, they often think that it is better to not "rock the boat" by sending their children to traditional schools where they will be exposed to methods of learning that they are not used to.

Three of the most common reasons as to why homeschooling is the choice for some families includes: Lack of religious instruction, unsafe school setting, or the child has a physical or learning disability.

In some countries, religious instruction is not included in the curriculum of public schools. In order to provide a holistic education, you need to enroll your children in a private school. Unfortunately, private schools can be very expensive, which is why some parents turn to homeschooling as an alternative. Location of the private school is also another factor; if it's too far away, the family may not be able to afford the additional burden of finding a place for their child to stay during the entire school year.

Recently, the occurrence of violence in schools has given parents nightmares about leaving their children. Terrorists and mad gunmen targeting schools and killing students have filled news headlines around the world. Because of this, some parents feel that it is better to educate their children in the safest possible place they know; at home, where they will always be within sight. Bullying and discrimination is also another reason why some parents opt to homeschool their children. Parents are protective of their children. You would not wish your own kids to have any bad experiences, especially when they are still young. Often, children who are homeschooled because of this reason are eventually sent to a traditional school setting once their parents feel that they are mature enough to endure being bullied or discriminated against.

If a child has a disability, it can be very difficult to learn in a traditional school setting. Often, a disabled child needs special care and attention that may not be available in traditional schools. Also, a disabled child often needs more time to understand his or her lessons and may not be able to keep up with the learning pace of the peer group. While there are private schools that provide the care and attention needed to help disabled children, not all neighborhoods have one. And if there is one within the vicinity, other problems such as financial obligations may hinder the child's chances of entering a private school. Disabled children are often targets for discrimination and bullying, so parents may try to find alternative education options. Lastly, there are parents who believe that they are the only ones who can provide the best care for their disabled child, including education, thus the choice to homeschool becomes an option.

Children in war-torn countries and places with civil unrest often get their education at home, because going outside would mean risking their lives. Schools are closed because parents would not allow their children to attend for fear that the school might be targeted or caught in a crossfire.

Sometimes, a family needs to move from place to place in order to avoid areas of conflict. Thus, a child would often receive an education wherever they go, so long as the family is together.

Those with special schedules, such as actors and athletes, are also often homeschooled. Homeschooling gives them the flexibility to adapt their education to busy schedules of work and training. Children of wealthy families are sometimes homeschooled. This is often due to security reasons, where parents prefer that their child would stay at home for fear of possible dangers, such as kidnapping and the likes.

Homeschooling is not for everyone, and not everyone who faces dilemmas like those mentioned above will find homeschooling to suit their needs. There are children who thrive by learning at home at their own pace without any of the distractions found in traditional schools. There are also those who do better when constantly faced with the pressures of the outside world. It is your job to weigh all the options presented to you before deciding to put your children in the educational setting of your choice. Remember that giving your children the best education they can have is a work in progress. If you find that one particular setting does not agree with your child's needs, then try looking for a different one until you find the setting that suits your family's situation.

How Much Does Homeschooling Cost?

For many families, the question of cost is a very important issue. While most parents aim to provide the best education possible for their children, there are other things they must also consider that is included in the family budget, such as food and clothing.

Private schools can cost a fortune as parents need to shoulder expensive tuition fees along with uniforms, school supplies, and other related fees and expenses. Typical private school tuition fees can range from $2,000 to $10,000 annually. Boarding schools cost more thanks to lodging fees and food expenses. Public schools, while generally free, still have hidden costs that can creep up during the school year such as field trips and project fees.

Homeschooling is nearly always a much less expensive option as compared to private schools. The thing about homeschooling is that it can either cost a family less than $100 per year, or more than $1,000 per year. The actual cost, more often than not, depends entirely on the parent. Parents can raise homeschooling costs by spending a fortune on curriculum, outside lessons, tutoring, equipment, supplemental books, and other teaching aids. However, you must remember that these expenses are made through your own decision. This means that while these expensive items may prove helpful to homeschooling your child, they are not mandatory.

Financially strapped families, wherein both parents are working, often believe that they need to make huge sacrifices in order to homeschool as one parent needs to quit his job in order to stay at home and teach their children. If a parent quits their job, then this means that there will be less income for the whole family because there will only be a single source of income. This problem is worse for single-parent families, because if the parent quits his or her job then there will be no source of income for the family. There are solutions to this problem, such as having relatives such as grandparents or an aunt or uncle who are currently unemployed to stay at home and supervise the homeschooling.

To give an idea of how much homeschooling can cost, here are a few options families can try:

The least expensive option is a public school program tailored to homeschoolers, which can be found in some countries that allow flexibility in acquiring needed materials. Some programs offer reimbursements when purchasing certain texts and materials that they recommend. However, if you decide to choose texts that are not recommended by the program, you may end up covering the cost from your own pocket. Other programs have a set, annual budget limit for each student. Anything over the budget is often shouldered by the parents as well. Some programs even offer to loan equipment such as microscopes and computers during the school term. There are also programs that provide consumable supplies, such as workbooks, papers, pens, and pencils that are often limited to specific amounts per student each school term.

For private homeschooling programs the costs will vary depending on the services they provide. Programs that sell complete curriculum packages may cost somewhere from $150 to $1,000 for a single grade. Some also provide extra support, such as guides and advisory teaching services for an additional cost. In some cases, these programs may require that materials such as textbooks and guides be returned upon completion of the course. There are also other programs that sell individual courses and books. Individual courses and books may cost around $15 to $50 each. Some homeschooling programs also offer discounts for every additional sibling enrolled, which can be helpful for families that have more than one child.

For those with tight finances, used homeschool curricula can also be found online, or join local homeschool support groups to see if they have curricula and materials that can be loaned or swapped. Free resources can also be found on the internet or at the local library. However, finding free or low cost resources and materials may take a lot of time, research, and patience.

Extracurricular activities such as sports, private lessons, and clubs can also have fees which can add to homeschooling expenses. However, there are also activities that are free or low-cost which can be found through local churches and recreational departments.

Chapter 7: 10 Tips For Teaching Reading

You hear it everywhere: reading is fundamental. One cannot get anywhere in life without the ability to read. Children learn to read in different ways and at different ages. By first grade, most children should be able to recognize letters and sound out simple words.

If you suspect dyslexia or any other learning differences, I would recommend you speak with a specialist. Do a Google search for dyslexia help in your area and go from there. You want to catch this early on before your child gets discouraged and starts saying things like, "I don't get it, I am stupid."

I have friends whose children started giving themselves those negative messages. The damage control on the child's self-image took longer than the actual therapy and exercises for dyslexia.

One thing I have heard over and over again from Christian parents of children with dyslexia is that they have their child read from the Bible for family worship, for their reading time in school, or both.

There is power in God's Word, no doubt. Even power to help a child with dyslexia. So I would definitely look into this as well, in addition to talking to a dyslexia specialist.

Otherwise, here are my 10 tips for teaching reading, whether your child has learning issues or not:

1. Relax, so your first grader can relax.

If you are stressed out and tense about it, your student will sense it in you. You don't have to tell him about your tension. It will come through your pores. Your child will feel it in your attitude, your tone and your actions. Actions speak louder than words.

So remember you are there to help your child, not to cram information down his throat. Forget all the negative people in your life who doubt your ability to teach your child how to read. Don't homeschool with their remarks in your mind, playing them back over and over. First of all, don't do that to yourself. Resolve your day will be positive and not dictated by nay-sayers.

2. Pick a curriculum which teaches phonics, not the whole-word method.

While you are at it, stay away from phonics textbooks with pictures, too. Children must make the connection between a letter and a sound. They don't need a third-party connection (a picture) to confuse them. Neither do they need an easy way out. If they are confused between d and b, of course the picture of a banana will bail them out.

3. Stay away from computer reading games.

It might seem easier to let them learn from a dancing teddy bear on the screen. They may be so fascinated with the colors, animation and the catchy tunes that they will not protest at all. You will be tempted to favor that over the moaning and groaning you hear as soon as you pull out a plain phonics book. Resist the temptation.

Kids will be kids. They will protest and show displeasure at learning activities. That's fine. Don't squash their feelings. You don't want to suppress their expression of dislike. You want to make sure you have an open relationship with them.

But they have to do their work. And it boils down to parenting. In my house, my children are allowed to voice an opinion and to present its merits. Sometimes I will let them negotiate me down to less than what I was asking them to do. And then, there are the five non-negotiables: devotional, school, piano, violin and chores. Once all these five get done, they get to pick their reward – most of the time, it's a 30-minute video. They know we do not allow more than 30 minutes per day of screen time and that it only happens if they finish their Fab Five activities.

Getting there was a process, especially when they were in preschool and kindergarten. By first grade, they knew what was expected of them and they did not protest too much or at all.

4. Understand that learning does not always have to be fun.

This retired public school teacher told me that she was appalled by all the emphasis on fun in the classroom. "I'm not for drudgery," she said, "but if you entertain children instead of teaching them in the lower grades, what will it be like when the hard work must be done in upper grades? Will you be singing algebraic formulas and calculus and physics problems all the way through high school?"

I think she has a point. There is something to be said about a pleasant teacher who understands the limitations of a six-year-old. A lively classroom décor, an inviting atmosphere, a welcoming and encouraging spirit – they all contribute to learning. But if all we do is entertain the children and make sure they have fun, they do not get challenged or stretched beyond their present abilities.

5. Don't be afraid to skip ahead.

If your child breezes through lessons, do two or three lessons a day. Some children read very well by first grade and there is no reason to hold them back. This is the whole reason you homeschool your child in the first place: to tailor his education to his interests and abilities. One of my children started kindergarten reading on a third grade level. By first grade, he was reading on a sixth grade level.

Our phonics program was so easy for him, I would do three lessons in a day. He would just read the text to me and I would explain some phonics or vocabulary. Then, we moved on.

6. Don't be afraid to put reading away for a few weeks.

If your first grader still has a hard time blending the letters together, even though he knows his alphabet, just give it a rest. Read to him. Play outside. Learn from nature. Go to the library. Go to the zoo. Take him to the playground and let him run around. Definitely remove the training wheels off his bike and let him figure out how to balance. There is research suggesting that graceful movements and coordinated physical activity affects cognitive ability.4

If your child enjoys art, provide lots of paper, crayons, markers, Do-A-Dot markers and worksheets and let him make art. It counts as school and it buys you time. His brain may need some time to process the latest lessons before it is ready to take in new ones.

Get back into it and press ahead for a few days. Is it easier? Is your child less frustrated? Sometimes immaturity keeps a child from learning or even making an effort. Children must be taught that learning takes effort and that it is not easy. When things get tough, the tough get going. Perseverance and grit can only be taught if you give your child a chance to struggle a bit.

7. Let daddy read to your child.

Reading habits are established early on and through repetition. Especially if you are teaching a boy, he must see the most important man in his life, his daddy, enjoys reading for himself and for his child. Daddy should absolutely avoid saying things like, "You are going to be a nerd" or "Don't read too much or your brain will explode" even if he feels like saying those things. On the contrary. Daddy should always emphasize the need for reading skills and that learning continues your whole life. A lot of professionals must go through continuing education classes. Everybody must do some form of reading every day on their job. Reading is fundamental and daddy must be on board with saying it and breathing it and living it.

8. Organize reading time with everybody in the family.

We like to read in the evening. It started out with a board book we read to our babies when they were two weeks old. By kindergarten, we knew we had read to them 1,000 different books. Were some of them twaddle, to borrow a term from Charlotte Mason? Probably. But guess what? They loved it. They loved being read to and they grew up to love reading.

It drew us closer as a family and it provided cuddle time. I know for a fact that my children's fondest memories have something to do with sitting close to their parents and reading books.

9. Go to the library at least twice a month.

If your local library does not have a story time program for lower elementary children, see if you could join the preschool program. Librarians are happy to have children in their building and they will make small adjustments to a reading program to appeal to all ages present. In our local library, there were several of us homeschoolers with younger children. The program was called Preschool Story Time and here we were with our eight-year-olds.

But the kids did not know this technicality. The librarian was happy to include some titles which would appeal to older children. She would also bring a stack of books along the same theme that we could check out after the program. And her crafts were always suitable to children ages 3-10. No problem. Eventually, they changed the name of the program, too. It is now called Preschool and Lower Elementary
 Story Time.

10. Turn off the TV.

This should have been the first item on the list. Brain research clearly shows how the habits created in the brain by TV watching make deep thinking and learning habits hard to establish. Watching TV is shallow mental work. If your child spends time building that habit of thinking on a superficial level, just taking in whatever he is being fed by the screen, reading will seem even more difficult and boring.5

TV is very fast paced and the attention span of children these days is a lot smaller than that of generations past because of all this TV watching. Give your child a chance and tame the TV beast. When your first grader grows up and performs academically well above his peers, he will thank you for being the "mean mom" on the street.

Chapter 8: What Is Homeschooling?

Homeschooling or home-based learning is the education of children at home instead of in a traditional setting, like a school. Parents usually act as teachers, but tutors can also be employed. The person providing instruction or mentorship is usually someone close to the child. Homeschooling is not a new practice, and many children were educated by their families or the community before the law made school attendance mandatory. According to the National Home Education Research Institute (NHERI), nearly 2 million students are homeschooled in the United States (2010). Home-based learning went from the 'norm', to virtually nonexistent (in the U.S. during the 1970s) to a legally-accepted alternative to traditional education at a rapid pace. While it's difficult to measure the effect of home education on academic achievement (due to the scattered population of homeschooled students, among other factors), studies on homeschooled kids and adults suggests generally positive outcomes. In general, homeschooled kids perform well in an academic setting and typically more likely to attend college in comparison to their state-schooled peers. They perform above average on standardized academic tests as well as on tests required for college admissions, like the SAT and ACT. In general, they are also self-motivated, well-adjusted and can relate well to people of different backgrounds and ages.

In the mid-20th century, religious groups like Mormons and the Amish homeschooled their children. It was only four decades ago that homeschooling was considered inadequate to satisfy the requirements of compulsory education, and those who persisted were fined and even imprisoned. Today, homeschooling is a legal option in all 50 states and in several countries. Modern home-based learning in developed countries like the U.S. is usually an alternative to education at private or public schools.

In the U.S., parents typically homeschool their children for the following reasons:

1) They are concerned about the learning environment

2) They find instruction in traditional schools inadequate

3) They want to provide religious or moral instruction to their children

Parents may also homeschool their kids while living abroad or to accommodate scheduling (many child actors/performers and athletes are educated at home). Sometimes homeschooling is the only option, for example families who live in isolated locations.

The number of homeschooled students in the U.S. is becoming more prevalent. Homeschooling reportedly saves taxpayers about $9.9 billion annually. There is a trend toward decreasing the burden of state requirements for homeschooling families, despite criticisms from advocates of traditional education. This educational phenomenon is quickly becoming what many are considering the 'best' option for their children.

Homeschooling Pros and Cons

Homeschooled kids have a reputation as self-directed learners and high achievers who go on to become productive members of society. You'll hear stories about homeschooled kids who score perfectly on their SATs and ACTs and get accepted to Ivy League schools. But that's only one side of the coin. Homeschooling is greatly a matter of choice, and it's not for everyone. Before you decide, consider the following pros and cons.

Advantages of Homeschooling

Less restrictive. Depending on the state, parents/tutors and students have more educational freedom. Usually, students get to choose what to study and how long they want to study it. It's all about customizing learning to the student's capabilities and maturity. Basics may be covered at an earlier age or at a later age. Parents also have more control over a child's daily schedule, and can plan events according to what works for them. Kids don't have to get up at the 'crack of dawn' to drag themselves to school (especially if they're not morning people); they can start learning when they are at their best.

Builds self-esteem. Peer pressure and regimentation are part of the experience in public and private schools. These can erode a child's self-esteem, particularly for middle-school girls. Homeschooled kids can act and think whatever they want without fear of upsetting others or not fitting in. Their lives are grounded by family and community, not by the opinion of other adolescents. Extracurricular activities that build leadership skills and cooperation also boost the child's self-worth, and prepare him or her for the real world.

Builds strong family and community ties. Homeschooled children spend most of their time with the family and community, promoting stronger bonds that may help check destructive behavior in rebellious teenagers and provide stability during difficult times. For example, going to several different schools can be disruptive when your job entails a lot of travelling. With homeschooling and an excellent curriculum, you can ensure quality education for your children wherever in the world you may be.

Freedom to practice religion. Many parents want to provide religious and moral instruction to their children, and find that homeschooling is the best way to do this. In fact, the homeschooling movement of the 1980s was born because fundamentalist Christians pulled their children from schools that they felt were not providing proper moral instruction.

Financial freedom. While homeschooling is not the cheapest educational option, and it is generally more expensive than sending your kids to public school, it is, however, cheaper than private school. If you are pulling your kids out of private school, homeschooling can save you a lot of money. Homeschooling means no daily drives to school, no uniforms, no brown-bagged lunches (or lunch containers) to buy, no expensive junk food and no trendy clothes and gadgets to help your child "fit in." One homeschooling mother told me that her biggest savings was on shoes. Not bad at all.

Disadvantages Of Homeschooling

Eats up a lot of time. Obviously, if you plan to homeschool your children, **you** need to be prepared for the time investment. You may realize that you can no longer work full-time, or your partner can no longer work full time. You may also find yourselves cutting back on time spent socializing.

Being around each other all the time. 24/7 "togetherness" can be suffocating, to you and to your child. If your child is naturally gregarious, independent and feels at home within a social circle, home study may cause loneliness and rebellion.

Can be expensive. Compared to public school, homeschooling can strain your budget, particularly if you are a single parent or if your partner has given up full-time work. But while it is usually more expensive than public school, homeschooling is still cheaper than private school.

Chapter 9: The Advantages Of Home Schooling And Road Schooling

Closer relationship with your child/children

Home schooling and road schooling provide perfect opportunities to bond with your child in a different context, one that enables you to know exactly what and how they are learning. You will also come to understand your child's learning style, which is invaluable for you, as their teacher, to know. You will get to see another side to your child.

Teaching what you want, how you want and when you want

You may be following your chosen curriculum closely or not, but you have the flexibility to choose. You have opportunities to integrate your teaching into a Project Based Learning strategy, which is explored later in this book. And you can integrate the environment you are experiencing, into your teaching.

Tapping into your travels – real-life learning

There are always going to be 'Teachable Moments'. Be aware of these golden opportunities to capitalise on learning. For example, there may be a heated 'discussion' in your classroom between your children. They may be doing a lesson on 'nouns.' Stop the lesson and discuss resolving conflicts, etc. You are actually capitalising on a real-life situation and the learning here is powerful because of timing and its relevance. I call this 'dropping the reins.' You can always come back to the lesson or make this part of the lesson! Capitalise also on the things you see and experience on your journey. A great springboard for further learning on the topic.

Creativity and imagination in how you present your teaching, assessment and record keeping

You have permission to be as creative as you wish – where else would you get this opportunity? It really is very liberating when you can put your 'stamp' on things! Expand your thinking in the planning and delivering and give yourself some time to do so. If you are following a curriculum, be creative how you approach this so you avoid being 'prescriptive' in your teaching.

Increased productivity

Because the 'school day' is based on quality not quantity, often you will find productivity is increased. We will talk about this later in a later chapter. I would suggest the typical Australian school day is exhaustingly long for children-especially the younger ones. Thank goodness many schools now have a long session of relaxation and meditation after lunch. Students when home schooled are more likely to receive higher quality instruction time than a student in a class of thirty children with a variety of learning, social and emotional needs. The demands on one teacher are immense!

Predictability and safety

Let's face it, bullying and anti-social behaviour is prevalent in schools and these behaviours are not restricted to public schools. Bullies are everywhere-and yes- there are many adults who haven't outgrown it yet either. For students, the results can be devastating and learning becomes much more challenging. Students need to feel safe in their learning environment to achieve success. Although some schools address this issue, the reality is that bullying is covert, and with students on mass in schools, it is sometimes very difficult to detect and therefore difficult to deal with. There are arguments to suggest that home schooling and road schooling hinder 'resilience building' by protecting students from bullying, However, from my experience, I would suggest the contrary. The experiences gained from home schooling and road schooling, I believe, empower students to a point where they are confident and resilient and have a highly evolved sense of self.

More rest and no homework-please!

Children need their sleep and if they are not bound to the normal school day routine, they are able to catch up on work when they need to. There is greater flexibility. And of course, they are not staying up late doing homework. This gives scope to work more with their bodily and seasonal rhythms which leads to better health and wellbeing.

More play in natural surroundings

If you are road schooling, your children will possibly have more opportunities to be connected to nature. Children become very resourceful and imaginative when they have limited things to play with. And what a gift it is to see what your children can create when there is not an overload of toys! This is a large topic in itself: Are we overstimulating our kids with too many toys and too much choice? For home schoolers as well, this is also the case as being at home allows more freedom and time to connect with nature.

More integrated learning possibilities

In the following chapters we'll look at ways you can integrate subjects by way of Project-Based Learning. This just means all learning of subject areas can be focused on one topic which makes learning more meaningful and purposeful.

Focus on learning not testing

Teachers in public schools, much to their displeasure, are increasingly becoming data collectors. As teachers, we long to be trusted to develop great relationships with our students and to implement great teaching. The time for teaching and learning is being increasingly spent on testing and data collecting. And for what purpose, I often wonder. Teachers need to be accountable but with the overload of external tests and assessments, undermines professionalism and credibility and reduces the time spent with students, working on this that matter. Like relationships, as an example.

Opportunities to be resourceful

Parents with whom I have worked have always been amazed at children's resourcefulness. When something is needed in the classroom and can't be accessed from a shopping centre, they improvise or just make what they need from what they have got. Any opportunity for your student to problem solve, should be strongly encouraged.

Using social skills in real-life situations

If you are travelling, look for opportunities where your child/children can directly interact with local people, for example by asking directions to get somewhere in a town that you are visiting. Asking a stranger directions to the local library is certainly out of some children's comfort zone. They also need to remember the instructions thereby developing memory and spatial geographical skills. Another example might be preparing and conducting an interview as part of a History or English project. The learning involved in this exercise covers many subjects and skills such as Oral and Written Language, History, Art, Communication skills, and so on. So, look for these opportunities where your children are 'putting themselves out there'. Needless to add, with a secure safety net!

Chapter 10: Spiritual Preparation For Homeschooling

God's Love: Getting together

You might be tempted to say, "Oh, I know that I am supposed to pray, and that will help. But what I really want is practical tips." I know that this is how I used to respond. But, the most practical way to homeschool success is to establish a personal prayer routine and Bible reading. Cross-stitch's motto is "A Day Hemmed In Prayer Seldom Unravels." Read on if you ever feel lost or overwhelmed.

Most of us don't spend enough time with God. It can feel like a busy mother or wife can find it difficult to find time for prayer. I used to console my self by telling myself that I would be one of those praying grannies, as I couldn't imagine myself having an uninterrupted hour of communion with my Lord Jesus until my children were grown and I was a grandmother. This lie was one that Satan told me for twenty years. Deep down, I knew I needed a prayer lifeline at this time in my life. I was still able to have my little ones. I did 'pray'. I offered small token prayers, little prayers of thanksgiving, and small 'bless you please' requests. But God only got my spare time and not my precious. I was guilty of daily prayerlessness and wondered why I felt so stressed.

What was the 'precious moment' that I needed to find and give God? I found the answer in scripture and especially Jesus' life. It is worthwhile to examine in detail how Jesus made prayer a priority.

Jesus experienced all the common weaknesses of the flesh while on earth, including hunger, thirst, and tiredness. He understood he had to find strength to face each day. Jesus was constantly under "people-pressure". These verses will help you understand:

Mark 1:37

". ". . They said unto him (Jesus), All men are looking for thee."

Mark 1:9-10.20

"And he spoke to his disciples that a small boat should wait upon him because of the multitude lest they should throng him.

He had already healed many, so they asked him to touch them.

The multitude gathered again and could not even eat bread.

Mark 6:31

"Jesus (Jesus), said unto them (the apostles), Come ye yourself apart into a desert area, and rest for a while: there were many people coming and going and they didn't have much time to eat.

Luke 12:1

". ". . There were many people, so that they could walk one after another. . ?.

The gospels are worth reading. These gospels show that Jesus was a high-stress worker. Imagine a crowd of over five thousand people following you around and clamouring to your attention almost every day. We find a whining toddler and a demanding teenager difficult to bear. . . Jesus felt pressure from the crowds and was also constantly threatened by His enemies. He also felt sorrow over the rejection of the ones He loved. These were major stress factors, humanly speaking. Christ Jesus was a very human man. However, just as the brakes on a luxury car, Jesus' humanity was 'power supported' by God through prayer. Jesus Christ, our example, prayed to receive the strength He needed to complete what He was sent to do. The same power is available to us.

So how did Jesus manage to find the time to pray? It wasn't that He found it; He made time for prayer. He made it a priority to pray so that He could spend at least twenty-four hours uninterrupted praying.

You say "Oh, I'd love to do that." It's impossible for me to fit it in. I understand. Tell me though, how many meals do you eat every twenty-four hour? Do you get six hours or more of sleep each night? Do you make time to wash your hair, take a shower, and get dressed? All these things are necessary for us to do. We don't shop in our sleeping clothes and then tell the shoppers we didn't have the time to dress for the day. Maybe we are 'undressed' when we start shopping without praying.

We all make time for what we believe is important. These examples demonstrate how important prayer was for Jesus.

Mark 1:35

"And in the morning he rose up a great deal before day and went out to a lonely place and there prayed."

Luke 6:12

"And it came about in those days that he went to a mountain to pray and continued to pray to God all night."

Jesus' attempts at being alone sometimes proved futile. Matthew 14:12-16 describes Jesus' attempt to be alone after hearing about John the Baptist's death. He then departs by ship for a lonely place to grieve. The crowds follow Him and He is soon moved by compassion to leave His own needs behind and help others. These scriptures were harsh to me because I was frequently moved by frustration rather than compassion when my children sought me out during my quiet times.

If we ask God, our loving God will always have the answer to all of our problems. For me, the answer was "rising up a great deal before day", something I believed I couldn't do. I couldn't do it in my own strength.

I was always slow in the mornings and very tired. Evenings were my best time and I was somewhat of a night owl. Yet, I didn't pray. Help came when I finally admitted my sin and asked God for His forgiveness. God now wakes me up early so that I can spend time with my Lord before the kids get up. Knowing that I'm still susceptible to fatigue, I make an effort to get to bed before 8pm to show the Lord I want to be with Him in the morning. Children are usually in bed by 7:30 at night, which is good for everyone. Our home has an evening Bible study and the children read aloud stories to each other. This means that I need to plan teatime for around 4:30 or 5. This works well for us because our husband is usually home at that time. Our main meal and the most washing up will be done at noon, rather than at the end. Simpler, lighter meals in the evening mean less washing up, more family time, and a quicker bedtime. God has a plan for you and your family, even if it is not the same as ours. Ask God for wisdom.

Although flexibility is great, it's best to stick to a routine with young families. Some people cannot do this because they work shifts, are home-nursing, or have other circumstances. Jesus had to be "instant in season and outof season", sometimes taking a special step to meet a special need. Have you ever wondered why Jesus told his disciples often to sail to the other side Lake Galilee? Even in the face of stormy weather? Jesus claimed that He had no place to rest His head. Sometimes, this was the only way to get away enough from the crowds to sleep. Only Jesus, who was physically exhausted, could stay fast asleep even as stormy waves swept over the boat (see Matthew 8;19-24).

Jesus understands our limitations. We should follow the example of the disciples and respond to His invitation to "Come aside and rest awhile", before we rip apart - at all seams! It might be time to take a step back when you feel stressed. Ask a friend or relative who is likeminded to visit your children and take you to their empty house to have a rest. Ask your husband if he would mind taking the kids to eat at a restaurant while you nap. Maybe a short walk by yourself will be enough to refresh you. These are the 'special steps' that will help you catch up and get back on track. You need enough rest for your body via sleep and enough strength for your spirit through prayer, just like Jesus.

"Charged" for the Day

Regular prayer is essential for any Christian. We need to recharge our spiritual and physical batteries. Second, we must hear from God what He has given us to do for His Master.

There are many resources available that can help you with prayer. We won't attempt to repeat their messages. Your prayer time will likely include the four elements of scripture: Adoration (Confession, Thanksgiving, and

Supplication) (A.C.T.S. We will not be able to see the requests or supplications you make for your homeschooling spiritual preparation.

You might consider praying for your spouse and yourself first, so that God would give you godly wisdom as parents. James chapter 1, verse 5, promises wisdom to all who believe. Ask God to show you areas of your home that are not in His order. Are you, as a wife, in Biblical submission to your husband. If God is trying to help us with a problem and we resist Him, He might allow us to have 'bad' days until He gets our attention. It is best to let God handle your spouse's situation if you feel that they are not following God's will. Be faithful to pray. If the Holy Spirit directs you, don't try to correct your husband about an issue. Be sure to listen to God's Spirit and not your indign flesh when he directs you.

Next, pray for your children individually and ask God to use the homeschooling activities that day to open their minds to spiritual things.

Children cannot be saved by their parents. However, we are instructed to raise them in the love and instruction of the Lord (Ephesians 6,4). This is Christian training. We are planting seeds and asking God for His blessings by training our children in God's ways and praying for them. Paul, the Apostle, gives us a picture of how we work together to harvest souls and build these lives on the foundation of Jesus Christ. It is the souls and lives of our children that we work the hardest for.

1 Corinthians 3:6-11

"I planted, Apollos watered, but God gave the increase.

Also, neither is he who plants anything nor he who watereth; it's God who gives the increase.

Now, he who plants and he who watereth are both one: each man will receive his reward according to his work.

We are all labourers with God. Ye are God's husbandry. Ye are God's building.

As a wise masterbuilder and according to the grace of God, I have laid the foundation. Let every man be careful how he builds thereon.

There is no other foundation than the one laid by Jesus Christ.

A fruit tree can grow and produce in unexpected places, even if no one planted it or watered. Children from non-Christian homes can also be entrusted to Christ by being trained and prayed for. It is clear that the best harvest comes from an orchard. Jesus expects us all to be faithful in watering with prayer the children He has given to us to train.

Encouragement to yourself in the Lord

You can avoid stressful situations by being like David in the Bible (1 Samuel 30:6). Prayer and praise are the best ways to do this. David's psalms include both of these elements. It's difficult to feel stressed while worshipping God in song. Your heart will sing along with your mouth, until it hums with joy. You can forget about the amazing things He has done for your life and focus on His wonder. You can also draw encouragement from God by reading His Word and inspiring books, magazines, or blogs.

A personal and methodical Bible reading plan is a good idea. You can read the Bible in one or two years if you use a scheme (see Chpt 19 Resources for more ideas). George Mueller, the man who provided for thousands of English orphans during the nineteenth century through prayer alone, stressed the importance of reading at least one portion of each testament daily. He gave each orphan a copy the 'Daily Light' scripture devotional to continue their daily relationship with God's Word. (See Chpt 19 on 'Resources').

If we are to be more like Jesus Christ, we must know how Jesus lived. This means that we should read the gospels often. It is important to reflect on what you are reading and to draw inspiration, insight, and comfort from it. A printed Bible study guide may be the best option, but I prefer a simpler method that I found once and modified to my liking. These steps will guide you through this method:

1. Next, write the date in your journal. Then pray and ask God for His wisdom today.

2. Take the time to read today's scripture section. This section will contain approximately 10 verses. It follows the previous day's reading.

3. Write down a title that best describes the section. You could use "God commands Noah to build an Ark." (Many

Bibles include their own headings. I prefer to create one for myself.

4. Write down a Key Verse. There is no right or incorrect answer. Just choose the verse that you think is most important or stands out.

5. Write down four key facts from this section. These are a summary of the events or a set of statements taken from the verses. You might discover something new or recollect an old fact. Although you don't need to interpret meanings, you may feel led by the Spirit to do so.

6. Write down a principle that you can apply to your life by praying over the portion. You might find it helpful to consider how Noah followed God's blueprint for the Ark. Imagine if Noah had believed that a 1-cubit window wouldn't ventilate vessels that large. What if Noah thought he had to change God's design? These thoughts might help you to apply the principle of "unquestioning

obedience" to your daily life. There are many applications that the Spirit can speak to you.

To facilitate inductive Bible study, a blank notebook can be created. However, if you'd like to buy a personal Bible Study Notebook with these steps, please see Chpt 19: "Resources". There are also versions for children and older adults. These make great gifts. The above Bible reading method will not get you through all of the Bible in a short time. You may need to set a daily schedule or listen to an audio Bible every day. Hidden nuggets can be found by meditating on a few verses at a time. This is something that's not possible when you read the entire Bible straight through.

These steps allow me to really think about the things I have read. It's like an archaeological dig scene. The entire site is marked out with string lines that cross at regular intervals. A student is found in each area that has been enclosed by string lines, and he or she sits there, unaffected by the heat, and brushes away at the dirt, looking for a tiny bit of ancient treasure. It is possible to find spiritual treasures by only focusing on a few verses at once. Bible study was once just an interesting hobby for me. It has evolved into something delicious.

Reading the testimony of others Christians who have experienced great stress and hardship can be a powerful encouragement to the Lord. When you read such compelling biographies, it becomes apparent that suffering for Christ brings joy and effectiveness in the gospel. We Christians have a printed legacy of the lives of Christians who persevered to bring others into God's Kingdom. Let their stories inspire, challenge and encourage you.

So, for example, I have to admit that I make great efforts to ensure the lounge room is warm and cozy when I get out of bed at night to pray. Recently, I read about a young Chinese student in communist China. She would often leave her dormitory to meet others on the snowy roof for their daily prayer meeting. If there was a blizzard she would grieve the loss of this opportunity to meet together, but then she would search for a cold corner to read her forbidden Bible. This girl's devotion challenged my comfort.

It is good for our souls to hear of those who sacrificed everything to advance God's kingdom. Think about Jonothan Goforth's wife and their gospel-bearing journey through China that left in its wake the graves of their children. Richard Wurmbrand is another example, who wrote about his years in Russian communism prison and torture, inspiring many to a deeper spiritual walk. Contact one of the hundreds upon hundreds of sending organizations to get involved in the daily struggles of missionary families. They can help you write encouraging letters to someone who is working for God in a difficult culture.

What will this all do for your stress levels and how will it affect you? It will help you see the big picture and put trivial things in perspective. Some Christians have been called by God to confront the outrages of Muslims against their children. Is He calling you instead to the endless sink of dirty dishes? Thank God! God will always give you the strength and courage to tackle the task He has given you. We must be patient with God and allow Him to prepare our spiritual lives.

It is important to adjust your values daily in light of the eternal issues. After attending an activity at a distant location, a dear friend who homeschools had just returned home with her children. My friend felt irritated and snappy about the children, it was after their normal lunchtime. The phone rang. The voice of her husband said that he had been calling home since the morning news about a road accident involving a family with a car similar to theirs. His relief was immense. My friend got up and gathered her children around her. She wept with her indignation at her inability to communicate effectively with her children. Her stress vanished instantly. Instead, she felt grateful to be alive and that she was the mother of five healthy kids. It could have been worse.

Keep our eyes on the eternal and remind ourselves that all the tasks God has given us today, no matter how tedious or overwhelming, are ministries. They are to be done as unto God. Interruptions, frustrations and other unpleasant situations will be seen as opportunities to show love and minister. Even though we can thank God for the trial He sent, we can also be thankful that He uses it for our spiritual good. A victory over a trial is an eternal victory.

This is possible only if we spend enough time in sweet communion each day with our Savior Jesus Christ, receiving from Him the peace that transcends all understanding.

Spiritual Preparation for the Whole Families

Homeschooling is an integral part of a family's lifestyle. It is vital to give spiritual encouragement daily to all members of the family. Family devotions (or family altars) provide an opportunity to do this and allow your children to "grow and know our Lord and Savior Jesus Christ" (2 Peter 3:8).

Our Devotions Time includes singing together, reading a Bible chapter (each person is reading a verse in turn), sharing from Daily Devotionals, and praying. We have used many spiritual exercises and activities over the years to keep it fresh and interesting. Participation is vital. Often, the children are asked for their prayers to be led by the adults. Family worship is a great way to thank God for answering prayers. Remember to pray for your homeschooling friends. You need their prayers, too. It might be possible to have a family Bible study or simply discuss the chapter together. (See Chpt 19: "Resources").

It is a good idea to start teaching your children to pray before they start any task. It's a good habit to start with your children when they are young and continue with them as you get older. This is something you want to be a part of their lives for the rest of your life. This will help them avoid future stress.

The Messenger Without a Message

What happens to our spiritual preparations for homeschooling? Some people homeschool without any prayer time. But others do it well. Non-Christians may be able to homeschool without any spiritual preparation. They define success as academic excellence or a successful career. While these are worthy accomplishments, they do not represent the main goal of a Christian family. Chapter One explains that we homeschool because God has called us to do so. We use this privilege to help our children grow in godliness and spiritual maturity. Do you want your children learn to trust Jesus Christ as their Savior? Your role is to guide them towards this relationship with Him. How can you pass on grace to your children if it is not something you have? You can't rely on books to do the job.

2 Samuel 18:19-33 tells of a runner who was sent with a message to King David about the day's battle. The commander granted permission for a second man to run, knowing that he could outrun the first. Although permission was granted, the fastest runner was not charged with delivering a message. Although the faster runner reached the king first in fact, the message was not delivered until the first runner to receive it.

Similar to the above, God doesn't care if your children finish the school year one grade ahead of their peers. Even though you might be the best homeschool mom, creative or intelligent, you don't have the message to convey. It is better to be slow or have a less impressive schoolroom than to have children who are constantly energized by the Master Teacher.

Chapter 11: Recent Growth & Acceptance Of Homeschooling

Homeschooling has increased significantly in recent years because many parents are starting to become dissatisfied with the way private and public schools are being handled. Education has always been important, and along with recent growth there has been more acceptance and guidelines added onto the idea of homeschooling.

The acceptance is making homeschooling much easier for different parents to try out, and it makes it easier for your children to succeed in this environment. Homeschooling is even popular for college students, but we're looking at grades K-12 in this book.

There are now support groups for parents that are homeschooling their children, standardized testing, and even books and videos that can help a parent start homeschooling their child, and it teaches the parent how to do it right. This way your child won't fall behind socially or academically.

Recent Growth:

Homeschooling was slow to take off, but it has sky rocketed since 1999, even though it started in the 1970s. Since 1999 in the US homeschooling has increased 75%. Though, nationwide only 4% of students are homeschooled. Still parents fear that homeschooling their children will put them at a disadvantage later in life, or even that they may not be able to give them the same education as traditional schooling options. These fears can be put to rest as standardized testing is starting to be made mandatory in all states.

It has even been proving that homeschooling will help kids score better on these standardized tests than anyone who has went to a traditional option such as public or private school. On average, kids who attend a traditional schooling option score within the fiftieth percentile, but children who have been homeschooled score in the sixty-fifth or higher. There are little to no achievement gaps when it comes to homeschooling, but there are many present in traditional educational options.

In traditional school options there are achievement gaps when it comes to poverty levels, ethnicities/races, and even sex. These gaps are not present in the percent of students that are homeschooled. There are no gaps separating anyone, and many would say that the playing field has been leveled in the home environment. When they hit the higher ages, such as high school students, homeschooled students are also known to score high on their SATs and ACTS, actually helping them get into college.

A common worry with homeschooling is that there will be no socialization for the child in question. However, that just isn't true. The amount of socialization that a homeschooled child receives is up the parent. There are now many social groups for children that are homeschooled because no one wants them to fall behind socially either.

Acceptance of Homeschooling:

Another fear of homeschooling your child is that they will not be accepted as part of a community or group, or even schools, because they've been homeschooled most or all of their life. Not only do many schools, including Harvard, accept homeschooled children, but socially they are accepted to. When they're going out at a park or shopping, you'll find no discrimination because they won't know if your child was homeschooled or not.

However, many people ask the question if there is a social difference between those who seek a traditional education and those who do not. There are still many people that will challenge the idea that homeschooling is preparing the children to be a part of the 'real world'. They will claim that the child is becoming isolated. Though, many people will argue that this assumption is backwards. Traditional school options are not preparing children like they used to or how they should, and they are not preparing them for the real world situations that a homeschooled child may be more aware of.

Homeschooling has a social acceptance now because they're more mentally prepared for the real world. Field trips are limited for those that follow a traditional educational route, but it is up the parent's discretion how many educational field trips that their child will receive. There are many companies and partnerships that are willing to let a homeschooled child into the premise without others in the group. This means that a homeschool child will be accepted to learn and have social applications to what they're learning even in the workplace.

For those that are in private or public school there is usually a problem of them following the foolish actions of their peers, but for those that are homeschooled they are more likely to follow the examples of an adult. Peer pressure is also no longer a problem when homeschooling your child. They'll be more accepted and ready for the adult world, including the college environment, because they were homeschooled.

Though, to really help your child develop even when being homeschooled, it is recommended that the parent help them join a social group. Many will join church youth groups, music lessons, or even sports teams. It's not recommended that any lessons be private, but music and dance will also give them an edge when it comes to college applications. For parents who are homeschooling their children, it is often easier for them to help their children participate socially in different and various activities.

The Advantage:

Homeschooled children have one-on-one time with their teachers because they are their parents. The parents will usually understand their problems when it comes to understanding the material presented better than many teachers. There are now social programs that have been made and specifically tailored to homeschooled students, but there are other groups that are open to the public that they can join in as well. Your child, if homeschooled, is less likely to fall into peer pressure, and it's more likely that they'll start acting like an adult at a younger age. The achievement gaps are nearly nonexistent within homeschooling, and many colleges will look highly upon it.

Chapter 12: Homeschooling Is Education That Is Tailor-Fitted To Your Children's Specific Temperaments, Body Clocks, And Learning Styles.

One of the main problems with current mainstream education is that it seldom takes the learning styles of students into consideration. It is rare that a teacher will take the time to figure out why a student excels in the arts but struggles with equations or why a student shows zeal in English class (working on an essay) but displays impatience in Chemistry class (performing experiments with a group).

Homeschoolers, on the other hand, rely on the knowledge of their students' primary and secondary learning styles to choose or create a curriculum that fully engages the students' minds and that makes sense to them. This ability to customize the children's education to their specific learning styles maximizes their retention of subject matter and makes learning much easier and more enjoyable for teacher and student alike.

Homeschoolers may also customize a curriculum that employs the different learning styles in an effort to address and improve a student's weaknesses. For example, if a child does well with visual learning, a homeschooler may gradually introduce physical/kinesthetic and musical/auditory learning delivery methods as well as visual. This allows the student to work on his or her weak areas while enhancing his or her strengths. Employing various learning styles (eventually and gradually) also prepares students for college instruction, which is mostly delivered in lecture format.

Homeschoolers also utilize knowledge of their students' temperaments to inform their teaching philosophies and methods. A student's temperament (whether sanguine, choleric, etc.) and how adults react to it affects the student's self-image and how he or she approaches people and tasks.

Homeschoolers also benefit from time freedom. A homeschooling family can work at time periods that fit with their life and preferences. This can allow them to enjoy a meteorological phenomenon one night and not have to be concerned with an early morning commitment that leaves them exhausted and less likely to learn. In addition, time freedom allows children to work at their natural alert time. Some children function better early in the day while others do better later on. Homeschooling allows the student to thrive during their study periods.

Education is not "one size fits all". When your child sits in a classroom with 30 other students every single day, how can it be possible for a single teacher to adequately meet each student's individual learning needs? How can a student vie for the teacher's attention? If the teacher barely has the opportunity to spend sufficient time with each of his/her students, how is he/she able to teach abstract concepts - such as dignity or sense of self - that cannot be taught within the prescribed class hour? These are just a few of the many challenges that students face in a conventional education system and that homeschooling liberates them from.

Chapter 13: How To Create Lesson Plans

You need to build a lesson plan for each child that you will homeschool for each school day that you have identified. The plan will determine not only the lessons you will teach your child but the schedule when you will teach the lessons all through the year.

As you build your lesson plan, you should always go back to curriculum that you have chosen for your child for the upcoming year.

Here is an example of a curriculum list for English and Math for a child on the **5th** grade level.

Subject	Teaching Materials	Curriculum Elements
English	Book	Visit the

including grammar, spelling, writing and literature	club	public library to loan books for the student to read, as required.
	Period study	•Frontier Living: An Illustrated Guide to Pioneer Life in America •The Revolutionary War Memoirs of General Henry Lee •Founding Fathers DVD •American

	Revolution Battles and Leaders	
Spelling	Sitton Spelling Source Book Sitton Spelling Workbook	
Grammar	Grammar: A Journey Through Grammar Land, Pt. 1	
Math	Math – 5th Grade Level	•Saxon 6/5 Math •Teacher's Edition •Student Edition •Solution

		s Manual
		•Facts Practice Workbook
		•Concept Posters

In the above illustration, you will note that there are a number of curriculum element for the English subject while there is only one for Math. The simplicity or complexity of your lesson plans will depend on the materials and the specific curriculum that you plan to use.

In the above example, the math curriculum is pre-algebra and the specific teaching materials that you should use have already been pre-selected. Normally, a standard curriculum like the Saxon Math comes with lesson plans that have been properly broken down to correspond with a particular school day. This is the simplest method since all you have to do is to chart each curriculum lesson to the specific day that you want to teach it.

But there are also instances, similar to the English curriculum in the above example, wherein you will have to work with several curriculum elements. Even the suggested teaching materials are not yet divided into handy lesson plans. As such, you can expect to work harder for these types of curriculum. To ensure that your child get through all of the elements of the curriculum within the school year, you will have to properly plan and organize your lesson plans.

Creating a Lesson Plan for a Simple Curriculum

Since you will be working with several curricula for your child, it is a good idea to first choose the simplest curriculum, like the Math curriculum above with only one element. To create a lesson plan, you simply need to identify the specific lessons that you will teach for each school day.

You can opt to you a computer spreadsheet or a lesson plan book in plotting your lesson plan schedule. Below is an example of 2-week lesson plan for the Math Curriculum:

Day	Date	Curriculum	Lesson #	Topic	Duration
Mon	Sep. 7	Math	Lesson 1	Sequences & Digits	60 min.
Tue	Sep. 8	Math	Lesson 2	Even and Odd Numbers	60 min.
Wed	Sep. 9	Math	Lesson 3	Using Money to Illustrate Place Value	60 min.
Thu	Sep. 10	Math	Lesson 4	Comparing Whole Numbers	60 min.
Fri	Sep. 11	Math	Lesson 5	Naming Whole Numbers Through Hundreds, Dollars, and Cents	60 min.
Mon	Sep. 14	Math	Lesson 6	Adding One Digit Numbers, Using the Addition Algorithm	60 min.
Tue	Sep. 15	Math	Lesson 7	Writing and Comparing Numbers Though Hundred Thousands, Ordinal Numbers	60 min.
Wed	Sep. 16	Math		Field Trip	
Thu	Sep. 17	Math	Lesson 8	Subtraction Facts, Fact Families	60 min.
Fri	Sep. 18	Math	Lesson 9	Math Test on Lessons 1-8	45 min.

You can then continue this process for the rest of the school year until you have accounted for all the lessons included in the curriculum. Make sure that you take into consideration the days which have already been allocated to other activities like field trip. Skip those days when plotting your lesson plans.

Creating a Lesson Plan for a More Complex Curriculum

The sample lesson plan below uses the English curriculum described above. As mentioned earlier, you will have to plan for and create "lessons" for each of the 3 curriculum elements (Grammar, Spelling and Literature). As you might have noticed, certain elements such as Spelling, already includes teaching materials with the specific lessons to teach while others, like the Book Club, does not.

Day	Date	Curriculum	Lesson #	Topic	Duration
Mon	Sep 7	English/Grammar	Lesson 1	Grammar Concepts	30 mins.
		English/Spelling	Week 1, Lesson 1	Words to Live By	30 mins.
		English/Literature (Reading for book club)		The Chronicles of Narnia, Chapters 1-2	30 mins.
Tue	Sep. 8	English/Grammar	Lesson 1	Parts of Speech	30 mins.

		English Spelling	Week 1, Lesson 2	Words to Live By	30 mins.
		English Literature (Reading for book club)		The Chronicles of Narnia, Chapters 3-4	30 mins.
Wed	Sep. 9	English Grammar	Lesson 3	More on Parts of Speech	30 mins.
		English Spelling	Week 1, Lesson 3	Words to Live By	30 mins.
		English Literature (Reading for book club)	Lesson 3	The Chronicles of Narnia, Chapters 5-6	30 mins.
Wed	Sep. 16	English Grammar		Field Trip	
		English Spelling			
		English Literature (Reading for book club)			

You can then continue this process for the rest of the school year until you have accounted for all the lessons included in the curriculum. Make sure that you take into consideration the days which have already been allocated to other activities like field trip. Skip those days when plotting your lesson plans.

How to Put Together the Lessons Plans for Several Curricula

It is ideal to incorporate a lot of music lessons, sports, field trips and other education activities into your child's homeschool program. If you do decide to do this, you should also incorporate these activities in your lesson plans. In the above examples, you may have already noted the field trip scheduled for Sep. 16. That means that no lessons for English, Math and other subjects should be scheduled on that date. But if you plan to ask your child to write a report on the field trip, you should have follow-up lesson plans for the field trip. Another option is to ask your child to do preparation work prior to the field trip like researching about some of the processes in the place that you will be going to. If that is your preferred approach, you have to incorporate those preparation activities into your lesson plan.

Apply the above techniques in creating lesson plans for all the curricula and subjects you have chosen for your child. When you are done with all subjects, you then have to merge all the individual lesson plans to one big summary for all of the subjects for one school year. Doing so will give you a complete set of lesson plans for each day. Below is an example of the combined lesson plan for English and Math.

		English/Literature (Reading for book club)		

Day	Date	Curriculum	Lesson #	Topic	Duration
Mon	Sep 1	Math	Lesson 1	Suspension, 3 Digits	...
		English Grammar	Lesson 1	Grammar Concepts	...
		English Spelling	Week 1 Lesson 1	Words to Live By	...
		English Literature (Reading for book club)		The Chronicles of Narnia, Chapter 1-2	...
Tue	Sep 2	Math	Lesson 2	Even and Odd Numbers	...
		English Grammar	Lesson 2	Parts of Speech	...
		English Spelling	Week 1 Lesson 2	Words to Live By	...
		English Literature (Reading for book club)		The Chronicles of Narnia, Chapter 3-4	...
Wed	Sep 3	Math	Lesson 3	Using Money to Illustrate Place Value	...
		English Grammar	Lesson 3	More on Parts of Speech	...
		English Spelling	Week 1 Lesson 3	Words to Live By	...
		English Literature (Reading for book club)		The Chronicles of Narnia, Chapter 5-6	...
Wed	Sep 10	Math		Field Trip	
		English Grammar			
		English Spelling			

It is possible that as you merge the different lesson plans for the different subjects, you will have to make certain modifications to account for activities like field trips, too little or too much class time and other interactions amongst the different lesson plans. You may learn that the total study time for one day entails too many hours or not enough hours to qualify as a study day. You should be flexible enough to adapt to such modification so you can create an effective full set of lesson plans for your child.

If you have more than one child to teach, you need to take into consideration the impact of one child's lessons on another child. There may be days when one child's learning activities may affect how another child will be able to finish his or her planned lessons.

You may think that creating lesson plans is quite a tedious task. I will be honest with you and say that it really is hard work. It will take you a lot of thought, effort and time to plan one whole school year for one child alone. The job will become bigger if you have to do it for two or more children. But you need to keep in mind that building the lesson plans is a vital part of any effective homeschooling program. You can find solace in the fact that the task will become easier and faster as you gain more experience, especially when you have already developed a good sense of your requirements for particular topics.

You will need to update your lesson plans.

Even if you think that you have created well-planned lessons, it is quite unavoidable that certain things will change as you begin to implement your lesson plans. It can happen that you discover other activities that you want to incorporate in your lesson plans. At other times, you may realize that certain lessons require more time or less time that you originally planned. On certain occasions, you may become sick and not be able to find anyone who can substitute teach for you. On those days, your planned activities will not get done. You need to adjust your lesson plans to take into consideration all these unforeseen circumstances so you can achieve your goals for the school year. It is ideal to spend a couple of hours every week (ideally during weekends) to review and revise your lesson plans for the coming school week. You can also use this time to document the homeschooling progress of your kids.

Chapter 14: Homeschooling Your Preschooler

Preschool is the easiest age group to homeschool as you literally do not have to do more than you normally do in a regular day. Most unschoolers and traditional schoolers agree that preschool requires minimal interaction with a set curriculum, if any at all.

Kids between the ages of 2 and 4 learn best through play. Playing allows your child to discover the world with their hands. Your classroom for the day can be your very own backyard in the sandbox or taking a trip to the grocery store with dad. Little ones are very observant and they will learn by watching you.

When you do decide to engage in activities such as the ABCs, colors, and learning a phone number, make sure to keep lesson time short, sweet, and engaging. You will find that a 4 years olds attention span in minimal and when you try to force a child of this age group to sit still and listen for too long they will become disenchanted with the concept rather quickly.

The best thing you can do for your preschooler is to allow them ample playtime throughout the day in varying situations. Spend time outside and count the apples on a tree or have them help you fold laundry to work on fine motor skills. Literally, anything can be a learning experience for a preschool child.

Some other ideas include:

Coloring a picture and focusing on "staying in the lines"

Playing a matching game

Reading a story with a parent or sibling

Making cookies with mom or dad

Exploring a box of buttons and counting them (4 year olds and up)

Singing a silly song

Making a special card for grandma

Helping to give the dog a bath

Practicing teeth brushing

Making a bed

You will be able to gauge what your child's capabilities are and what they enjoying as the school year progresses. Although preschoolers love to keep, busy, do not forget to make time for napping and snacks. You will appreciate these little breaks too!

Chapter 15: Invaluable Resources: Homeschool Conventions, Co-Ops, Camps, Leadership Schools

Homeschool Conventions are ideal places to expand on your research. Even though I have been homeschooling for fourteen years, I still enjoy attending conventions because there is always new curriculum, new methods, and new connections to be made. You never stop learning, right?

I sent my firstborn to college last fall and the convention that I attended before her graduation gave me some amazing information and resources for transitioning her from home education to college. The Teach Them Diligently convention was offered in three states this year. This convention may not be available in your state, but a quick internet search will help you find one in your area. Thanks to so many veteran homeschoolers who have blazed the trail before you, there is a high demand for these conventions and for companies to produce curriculum.

Most conventions include lectures in various areas. These lectures can be informational, question-answer sessions, or inspirational. Of course, the curriculum fair is my favorite part because I can seek out the curriculum that I have been researching online and physically flip through the pages. I can spend hours thumbing through books and examining the layout of the curriculum and how the subjects line up with the learning and homeschooling styles in our family.

Homeschool Co-ops are groups of families who meet together to share knowledge and reach common goals. Generally, co-op groups are designed around a particular homeschooling style (Charlotte Mason, Eclectic, Montessori, etc.) Co-ops can be formed around academics, service work or projects, social groups, the arts, or extracurricular activities. In most co-ops, parents teach in the subject of their specialty or greatest interest. For example, I often teach in the areas of History or Language Arts. I really love American History and I never grow tired of writing or literature. This is the beauty of a co-op. If you have strengths in certain areas, go and share that in a classroom with other families. In return for your efforts, the other parents will teach the subjects that may not be your strength. It is a wonderful trade and your child will have an enthusiastic instructor instead of a parent who is frustrated by a subject that they struggle to enjoy. (That is math for our family.) Some co-ops meet once a week, others may meet more often. This is decided by the families within the group. Once you connect with some homeschoolers in your area, they should be able to point you in the direction of local co-op groups.

Camps – Summer Camps may be the first thing that came to your mind and many are available such as band, art, or music camp. However, because homeschoolers have a flexible schedule, camps are also available throughout the school year. The possibilities are endless and be aware that many of the educational centers and local attractions will offer lower rates for large homeschool groups. Don't be afraid to approach management and ask for discounts. If you are bringing in a large group during their slowest business hours, they will bend over backwards to accommodate you. An added benefit: most of the time you will have the place to yourself!

Leadership Schools – Speaking of a great activity available during the school year, one of our greatest finds as a homeschooling family was TeenPact Leadership Schools. The program is held in your state's capitol and provides unique opportunities to visit the key government buildings, meet politicians and lobbyists, and observe the government in action. At TeenPact, students are trained to understand the political process and engage at the local and state levels. The program is intentional about raising up the next generation of leaders. My second daughter loves history as much as I do and she began showing an interest in politics. When a friend told me about this program, I jumped at the chance to get involved. She fell in love with TeenPact! For two consecutive years, I helped chaperone a group of amazing teenagers as they gained knowledge and confidence by being immersed in their state's government and law making process. We both gained lifelong friendships and treasured memories from this experience. This is just one example; I encourage you to research what is available in your area. If you join a co-op, the director should be able to recommend options as well.

Chapter 16: Guidelines For Discipline In Homeschooling And Teenagers.

One of the most important aspects for home schooling is maintaining discipline and as the child gets older it becomes more and more difficult. Children are apt to take chances when the parent is their teacher, and what will add to making it difficult, is them being at home.

This makes schooling feel like a long summer holiday and to prevent this proper ground rules must be put in place from the beginning. I have mentioned a few times flexibility when it concerns home schooling and this can be used to your advantage.

Create a schedule for learning, when there are outdoors activities, and when examinations and testing will be done.

Use your discretion to design a proper timetable and enforce it with no exceptions. This is the only way to create a proper learning environment.

During the development and learning process of child they will need to understand how important it is in being polite and courteous, being punctual and having good manners.

If possible allocate a certain area of your home for education and studying so that an association can be made by the child.

22.

Think about what sorts of punishments you will apply if the child does not obey the rules, but make sure that the punishment suits the crime so to speak.

Do not let learning become an extension of play time while home schooling and make rules about being neatly dressed, and arriving at the desk or place of study on time.

Patience is necessary when teaching children discipline in home schooling and even more is going to be necessary when it concerns disciplining teenagers.

Homeschooling and Teenagers

When children reach the milestone of becoming teenagers parents have some misgivings about home schooling.

Some parents even change their minds and allow the teenager to go to a public school which ends up completely defeating the object.

Even I almost threw in the towel when my teenage daughter became argumentative, broody and at other times loud and rowdy...

Before you make such a drastic decision think about all the good you will be undoing by sending your teen to a compartmentalized education process which you did not want for the child in the first place.

23.

Home schooling teenagers can be even more rewarding if you work together because at this stage the child will have a better understanding about why you chose this option rather than public schooling .

Your social concerns should not worry you because there are many societies, clubs and associations that teenagers can join and interact with others and make new friends.

They will still not have to endure peer pressure, nor enforced subjects' education, which is the case at most high schools

With concerns about higher subject level education simply lean more towards tutors for certain subjects that are beyond you.

In my case I shared tutors with other mums that had children the same age and it worked out just fine.

Look for support groups in your area and you will be surprised to find there are many which will be perfect for helping teenager develop into self motivated able young adults.

The growth in home schooling all over the world now makes it simple to source interactive groups of other home schooled children and young adults, and the internet is a starting point to find those in your locations.

Remember the basic rule of home schooling which gives you as the parent freedom to help your child develop and grow in a stable environment.

At the same time you guide them to develop the necessary skills they need to enjoy a balanced successful life in a choice of careers that suit them.

24.

General Home Schooling Guidelines.

If you have read my guide this far you may have decided that you are going to choose home schooling for your child or children and if so below are some easy to follow guidelines that have helped me make home schooling a success.

Home schooling is a learning process for parents and a lot of trial and error is the norm with the first child. Smart preparation is the way to achieve home schooling success and today there are so many tools available to help you.

Kick off by investigating your country laws regarding home schooling and check that it is ok with the national education department.

See what can be found in the way of curriculums for the different grades and the easiest way to do so is investigating this online. Find out access to home school support groups in your area which can also be done using the internet.

Software and tools for progress recording and assessment are vital as mentioned before so get the best you can find which are also the simplest to use. Here again you will find the internet to be a superb resource.

Stationary books, art and craft materials and accessories can be purchased at the local store and your own discretion can be used to choose what you need to begin with.

Make a few notes regarding schedules, and how you plan to enforce disciplines. There are a few simple key pointers regarding this as follows:

1) Instill an eagerness to learn in the Childs discipline.

2) Show rewards for the child's hard work and efforts.

3) Stick to a Basic Routine

4) Maintain regularity in education times.

25.

5) Don't be afraid to make changes and stay flexible

6) Motivate, reward and show enthusiasm.

7) Practice patience

8) Listen to suggestions your child makes about home schooling.

Remember that flexibility gives you infinite possibility to educate your children which means you do not have to educate them 8 hours a day.

You also do not have to force the issue regarding subjects and skills but rather focus on developing their unique skill set.

Home School Structure for the Year

Now that your child is studying at home there is no need to stick to the same terms and school times. Flexibility is now yours remember so use it to everyone in the family advantage.

Vacations can be taken when it suits the family not the way it would be when children are attending public and private schools.

The curriculum you design is also not set in stone as we have stressed a number of times, so you can keep things interesting which maintain an enthusiasm to learn in your child.

It takes a bit of time to start falling into a pattern during home schooling and eventuality this becomes comfortable for everyone.

Higher grade subjects can be done by tutoring and you and your child can look out for suitable teachers that everyone feels comfortable with.

Plan extra mural activities and outings that allow your children o interact with others including children their own age whenever possible.

Coincide vacations to allow a little time off during summer breaks and holiday periods at the same time public schools have these breaks, otherwise children can become restless knowing that everyone else is on vacation while they need to study.

26.

Proper evaluation at set intervals during home schooling is not negotiable as this allows you and the children to see how they have progressed in home schooling while it also allows you to see where weaknesses are present and address these.

In a little while after starting home schooling a pattern starts emerging allowing parents to see what works and what does not and adjustments can be made to ensure the process of educating children at home provides the benefits that come with it.

Chapter 17: Routines For Homeschooling

When one decides to homeschool, there is so much to consider that it is easy to feel overwhelmed. Along with being overwhelmed, you may feel confused about what to expect. How will homeschooling affect your daily lives?

For some people, a set schedule is the best way to homeschool. For others, however, having everything planned out in fifteen minute increments doesn't sound like fun. Where structure might be desired, it isn't always practical. Conversely, while being relaxed might be great, some structure might be needed to be effective as a homeschooling parent. Much of it depends on your child and what would motivate your child to learn.

Here are the three different approaches you have in homeschooling your child:

1. Have a set schedule. School at home would have the children keeping a similar schedule as those in public school. This would include getting up at a specific time every day and then starting their day with either breakfast or chores as the first order of the day. Following that, the children would be given 45 minutes per subject, just as if they were in public school, and they would have a printed schedule to go by for their day.

2. Have a relaxed routine. If you're not enthused by this approach, a more relaxed routine might be more what you're looking for. If this is the case, you may start your day whenever one of the children gets out of bed. You can work with that one child, undisturbed, until the other children make their presence known. This type of routine would be more staggered, with mom giving special attention to each child as they rise.

3. Have complete flexibility. Some homeschoolers don't really have a set

schedule or routine for actual schoolwork. They may allow the children to choose which subject they want to do first, and continue in that way until all subjects are covered. This type of routine is great for those students who are self-starters and can work without supervision.

While these routines might be helpful, there are the people that are completely against anything planned and live life by the seats of their pants. This is the type of person that allows the day to happen to them, taking each moment as it comes and living their life to the fullest. They often have more fun, but may have a little bit of a problem finishing projects and school work.

Whichever routine or schedule you choose to follow, just remember that all work and no play make Jack a very dull boy. Take some time out of your scheduled day to enjoy your children. Plan some free time on your calendar to allow them to just relish in being a child. After all, part of the reason you chose to homeschool was so you could spend quality time with your children. Let the schedules and routines slip every now and then. You'll be glad you did, and your children will thank you for it.

How to Make it Easier for Parents

Homeschooling, while it affords you certain freedoms when educating your child, is not always easy. But there are things that you can do to make homeschooling easier for yourself as a parent. The following tips may help make your job as a homeschooling parent a little easier.

If in doubt, look on the internet. If you are in doubt about your method of homeschooling, use the internet to seek another method. In fact, you can use the internet to help you in regard to nearly everything homeschool related. If you are want to use games as a way of teaching your child math, language, and critical thinking skills, the following games are good to choose from: Checkers, Dominoes, Scrabble, Clue, Monopoly, Yahtzee.

Choose a complete curriculum. Complete curriculums will also make homeschooling easier on you as a parent. Instead of having to search through multiple catalogs to find just the right curriculum, choose a complete curriculum. Not only will it save you time, it may even save you money, in the long run. As the author of this guide, I will provide a complete homeschool curriculum based on your child's needs and grade level at a very reasonable cost.

Cut yourself some slack. Don't expect yourself to be the perfect teacher. Unless you have an education degree, you most likely will make mistakes along the way. Don't beat yourself up about them. Learn from the mistakes and try not to repeat them again.

Allow your children to help themselves. You can't be expected to know everything, so if your child wants to learn something you don't know, give them the freedom to follow their interests. You might be pleasantly surprised to find that they learn more on their own than they did while you were more involved.

Seek the help from others. When in doubt about anything dealing with homeschooling, seek the advice from those who have been homeschooling for longer than you. Even though they may not have dealt with exactly what you're dealing with, chances are they will be able to give you advice or point you in the right direction. Take advantage of your homeschooling peers' offers of help, there might be a time where you'll be able to return the favor.

Online communities are available. If you don't know people that homeschool in your local area, there are literally hundreds of homeschooling communities on the Internet. Search online for homeschooling groups or forums. They can be found in every state, and even some outside of the United States. You may have to register to join a homeschool group or forum, but you can be as active as you like and remain anonymous if you like.

Homeschooling doesn't have to be hard. In fact, one of the reasons most people choose to homeschool is the ease and freedom associated with it. When you have difficulty, however, you may feel as if you need help. The above tips, when followed, can help make homeschooling a little bit easier.

Chapter 18: Parents Are The Best Role Models.

The child learns what he wants to know. Parents have no problem facilitating the processes of dressing, using a fork, tying shoes, and, finally, a tremendous set of skills that the child has already acquired before going to school. And why do we think that you cannot learn to read in the same way?

The truth is that if we have patience, if we wait for him to be interested, and we strive to create opportunities that offer him the need to know, the child will learn everything he needs at every moment.

In addition, we must keep in mind that skill will be more important to one than another, depending on the focus of their talent or natural ability. The one who is going to be a writer will have to know the details of the grammar, but not the painter or the mechanic. The one who is going to be an astronomer will have to understand mathematics well, but perhaps it will not be of much importance to the poet.

It is also important that we, as parents, show the skill that we want to model for the child since the example and encouragement that we offer are the two most valuable tools for learning.

Let's not forget that no one learns to walk to receive a grade or to pass the other course. You learn to walk to get somewhere. In the same way, the child who realizes how interesting the stories in the books are will surely make an effort necessary to acquire reading skills. On the other hand, children who lack the experience of listening to stories read by their parents will find it difficult to become interested in reading even when the teacher is concerned with teaching them.

Knowledge. Knowledge is not learned by repetition. In the past, children had to recite the data they wanted to teach them. And what happened? When completing the exam, everything was forgotten. The dynasties of Europe, the table of the chemical elements, the Latin verbs, the capitals of the countries (many of which have been changed since then) — all this information is not knowledge

Knowledge consists of data organized in a useful way, that is, not organized in a book or curriculum but organized about the understanding of the individual who wants to learn it. As we said at the beginning, the mind is dedicated to seeking design. If you understand the design of chemistry or geography, it will not be important to memorize it all to know it. And let's see that each person is going to have it organized in a different way. For example, in school, perhaps we learned that Afghanistan was located near India, but in reality, little was known about it. Now, after the attack on the Twin Towers, everyone knows a lot of facts about this country. At the moment of meaning, knowledge is acquired effortlessly.

Parents who want to help their children acquire knowledge just take advantage of the opportunities that life presents them. If granny is going to have surgery to correct her eyesight, there is an opportunity to talk about optics, the anatomy of the eye, and the profession of a surgeon. Did the girl cut her finger? Opportunity to make a diagram of the blood circulation or read something about first aid. Did they find a spider in the yard? We go to the library to look for the name. This form of knowledge is never forgotten.

The brain is not simply a bottle waiting to be filled. Nor is it like an all-absorbing sponge. It is a very complicated organ that helps us differentiate between what is important and what is not. But if we let teachers make these decisions, we have already looked down on it. Soon the child will not have the ability to learn correctly, looking for the design that has meaning for him. Therefore, it is important that parents not only protect their children from this form of education but also that they do not incorporate them themselves in their efforts to educate them.

Summarizing then, how do you ensure that children acquire a basic skill? First, you need to determine if you are ready to learn it. Maturity is needed, perhaps some experience, and sometimes other prior skills. Second, the model is needed, especially from the parents. Third, some reason is needed: because it is useful. It interests you because it can help you in some way. Fourth, the child must possess an aptitude for such a skill. Just as some will never be able to play a musical instrument, others will not be able to understand algebra.

And how do you get the children to acquire enough knowledge? First, the most important thing is to answer the questions. When children are asking questions, it is precisely when they are learning. Second, the information has to be relevant related to your experience. Third, it is necessary to provide reference tools, be it maps, dictionaries, and encyclopedias, for example. The text that the father used in college can help the son to find answers to her questions.

Think of it like this: A wall is being built. Each brick is a fact, and the cement is the experience that unites and supports the entire wall. This type of education is invaluable and will not be missed when summer arrives. It is the education of the wise, of the leaders, of those who know and know that they know it.

Chapter 19: Homeschooling - Are There Other Options?

You have the option of sending your child to public school, private school or keeping them home for schooling. If you decide on either of the first two, you'll receive quite a bit of information before school starts from your district. If you are thinking about homeschooling for your little (or big) ones, you have to start now.

The first things for consideration are the rules and regulations of your state, city, and county. Call your local Board of Education to find out what their requirements are for homeschooling your children. I'm sure the laws have changed since my children were homeschooled. Some districts have quite a bit more oversight over what, and how, you can teach your child at home. In some states, parents may need to have a Bachelor's degree, while others states only require a high school diploma for you, the teacher. Find friends or neighbors that are homeschooling and network your ideas and resources. There are many home school conferences and associations that will guide the novice through every avenue of teaching your child at home.

There can be a major expense with homeschooling if you live in a stricter district. New books can be expensive for anyone, whether for you or the school district. Some areas will let you use library books and/or books you already have. Check out your local home school book sales where you can pick up text books for a fraction of the price. Some districts may loan you the books for school, if you are a tax payer in their district. These districts may be few and far between, but always check. It never hurts to ask, and it may save you some money.

For those subjects you don't feel qualified to teach your child, find others with the necessary skills. There are home school books publishing companies that have options for video learning with a qualified teacher. Music could be taught by a piano teacher. There are also home school associations that you and your children can participate in field trips and science explorations. Even some local community colleges will let high schoolers participate in college programs. Other districts will let your homeschooler's participate in athletic programs. My daughter was able to try out for, and play on her JV softball team, and both of our children took art classes at the community rec center. You really do have a lot to choose from.

If your choice is home school, you will need to get your lesson plans set up; books lists turned in, and get yourself organized. You can find all of your planning materials at a local school supply store. They have an abundance of lesson planners, maps, workbooks, flash cards, history time line charts, bells, rulers, paper, educational posters and everything in between. All of your lesson plans, book lists, and time lines will need to be submitted to your Board of Education. You have an allotted amount of time daily that you must spend on school work. At the end of the year there are assessment tests that need to be taken to make sure that your child is meeting up to the tasks.

Homeschooling is not for everyone. You know your child better than anyone, and your child knows you too, and how to push your buttons. You must be devoted to his education, despite the irritations that may arise.

ARE HOMSESCHOOLED KIDS SUCCESSFUL?

In actuality, they can be more successful!

What are the top reasons for homeschooling? Teaching your children yourself, at home, was widely despised just three decades ago, but is now becoming part of mainstream American culture. It is almost becoming fashionable to homeschool nowadays. And homeschoolers are no longer considered the lepers of society.

Back in the 80s and 90s, the main reason for homeschooling was religion. Parents felt that the secular education given in public schools ran counter to their own religious beliefs.

In the 21st century, many other parents are homeschooling their kids for various reasons. But homeschooling is not a recent phenomenon. Homo Sapiens have been homeschooling their kids for as long as they have been around, and that has been for a staggering 195,000 years!

But if you get the impression that homeschooling can never be on par with public-school education, you might be amazed to learn that some of America's distinguished presidents have been homeschooled. Whatever their reasons for homeschooling, the parents of George Washington, John Quincy Adams, Abraham Lincoln and Franklin Delano

Roosevelt would have been immensely proud of their children's colossal accomplishments.

Homeschoolers are no pushovers when it comes to intellectual achievement either. Research has shown time and again that homeschoolers consistently score higher on standardized tests than their peers educated in public schools. And homeschoolers are regularly gaining admission to the top universities of the world. Harvard, Yale, Stanford, MIT, Cambridge and Oxford (to name a few) have no qualms about opening the doors to their hallowed halls to armies of homeschoolers.

Home school statistics indicate that children who are taught at home receive higher scores on their standardized tests than children who are taught through a public school. The point average for homeschoolers was, in some cases, almost 70 points higher than the national average for public school children. This is a positive indication that individual teaching time makes a difference as does a quiet environment to study in. In home discipline is also important in being able to study in a more controlled environment.

Some of the brightest minds on earth such as Thomas Edison and Mark Twain have also been happily homeschooled. In short, one of the reasons for homeschooling is that your child can reach the dizzying heights of Mount Achievement.

But how do homeschoolers achieve such spectacular success? It is quite simple, really. Imagine a typical public school classroom. The harried teacher has to impart knowledge to the best of her ability to a class of between 20 to 40 kids with myriad personalities, backgrounds, hopes, emotions and IQs.

Only a person who has ever taught such a diverse group before will know how frustratingly difficult it is to make every one of them succeed. The chances of making every child succeed and go to college are almost infinitesimal. If you don't believe me, just look at the national statistics on failures and school dropouts in America. It is a dismal situation.

I am not blaming the teachers though. It is certainly not their fault. They are not miracle workers and should never be made into scapegoats for this appalling situation.

So what do public schools lack that home schools have in abundance? The answer is the precious commodity Time.

While public school teachers have no time to attend to the needs of each and every child in their class no matter how desperately they may want to, homeschooling parents have all the time in the world to answer all the questions of their children and make sure they fully understand the topic before moving on to the next. Unlimited individual attention is the trump card that homeschoolers wield with devastating force.

Conclusion

I hope this book was able to help you to learn all you need to know about homeschooling children.

The next step is to manage and maintain a good student-teacher relationship to ensure that your home school is effective.

It'd be greatly appreciated.

www.ingramcontent.com/pod-product-compliance
Lightning Source LLC
Chambersburg PA
CBHW071840080526
44589CB00012B/1075